THE
IRISH EMPIRE

~ THE ~
IRISH EMPIRE
PATRICK BISHOP

THOMAS DUNNE BOOKS
ST. MARTIN'S PRESS ∞ NEW YORK

*To my mother Kathleen Bishop, née Kelly,
and in memory of Philip Major R.I.P.*

THOMAS DUNNE BOOKS.
An imprint of St. Martin's Press.

THE IRISH EMPIRE. Copyright © 1999 by Patrick Bishop.
All rights reserved. Printed in Italy.
No part of this book may be used or reproduced in any manner
whatsoever without written permission except in the case of
brief quotations embodied in critical articles or reviews.
For information, address St. Martin's Press,
175 Fifth Avenue, New York, N.Y. 10010.

ISBN 0-312-26527-1

First published in Great Britain by Boxtree,
an imprint of Macmillan Publishers Ltd.

First U.S. Edition

10 9 8 7 6 5 4 3 2 1

The Irish Empire is based on the international television series 'The Irish Empire' co-produced by Little Bird, Café
Productions and Hilton Cordell Associates for RTE Television, BBC Northern Ireland and SBS Independent
in association with the Australian Film Finance and the Programme Rights Company.

Half-title page: **Landscape of County Mayo** *c.* 1890.
Title page: **New York stock exchange.**

CONTENTS

Introduction

This is the story of one of the great triumphs of the human spirit. It tells the tale of how the people of a small, poor nation, moored at the edge of Europe, spread themselves throughout the world winning power, wealth and fame. Over centuries, emigrants fleeing political and religious oppression, poverty and lack of opportunity turned the experience of exile into a sort of victory. Fate had prevented them from fulfilling their destiny at home. So they took their dreams and their identity elsewhere and built an empire overseas. An Irish empire.

This last phrase first occurred to me when I considered the extraordinary geographical spread of the Irish diaspora.* There are few areas where you do not find the traces of Irishmen and women or their descendants. They have left their mark on thousands of towns and cities, great and small, around the world, at the furthest extremities of the American continent, in the wilds of the Australian outback and the pastureland of New Zealand, in West Indian paradise islands and grand French manor houses. Extraordinary, too, is the sheer volume of the Irish scattering (to use the evocative term of Piaras Mac Einri of the Irish Migration Studies Centre in Cork). We will never know the true figure but the former Irish president Mary Robinson spoke in her inaugural speech of 'over seventy million people living on this globe who claim Irish descent'.

But the factor that convinced me that the phrase was appropriate was the manner in which the Irish transported their Irishness with them, nurturing it and sustaining it, demonstrating a devotion to the retention of identity that equalled that of Jewish immigrants. Time, the continual rubbing up against the culture of the host nation and communities, intermarriage — all of these things might be expected eventually to erase an awareness of ancestry in the generations that succeeded the original immigrant. But no. As Mary Robinson's statistic shows, an astonishing number of people in the world, no matter how remote in time and distance they may be from the island of Ireland, regard their Irishness as a part of their being and identity.

*The phrase was also used in 1917 by Archbishop Darcy, primate of All Ireland, who spoke of the British Empire as being also an Irish Empire on account of the number of Irishmen and women in its ranks.

A hard-won respectability: young Irish-American men and women at the Monaghan Men's Dancing Class in New York City, 1905.

Emigration meant betterment, according to this optimistic engraving of 1854.

Thus, without declaring war on anyone or seizing the territory of others, the Irish nation has managed to achieve many of the basic goals of imperial activity. They have found *Lebensraum*, wealth and power. In the process they have propagated their ideas and culture, spreading far and wide a notion of Irishness. What 'Irishness' constitutes exactly is not easy to say and is the subject of much scholarly and popular debate. By and large, though, the Irish convey — these days at least — a benign and positive image that sits well with the spirit of the times. That it was not always so is another story for the Irish to take pride in. They can derive some satisfaction from the fact that the Irish stereotype has lost its associations of drunkenness, ignorance and violence, to be replaced by sociability, creativity and a highly developed sense of humanity.

This notional Irish Empire, then, has given Ireland and the Irish an importance they would otherwise never have had. The political, religious, social and economic dynamics that drove the continuous depopulation ensured that Ireland's name was heard in the world in a way that other small northern European nations of equal size and population were not.

There were of course, many countries in Europe that exported their natives around the world, and particularly to North America, in the great migratory movements of the nineteenth and early twentieth centuries. But, proportionately speaking, more Irish people left, more often, than their counterparts in Britain and on the continent.

As the historian Donald Harman Akenson observes:

> More than any other European nation, Ireland in the nineteenth and twentieth centuries was characterized by emigration. In relation to its size, it lost more of its population through out-migration than did any other major nation. Most young Irish men and women who came into adulthood from 1815, the end of the Napoleonic Wars and the effective start of the great outward flood, until the present day, have had something in common: they have considered whether or not to leave Ireland.

Most have stayed home, but, as Professor Akenson points out, taking this decision has been as much a matter of conscious choice as leaving. In poor parts of what was already a backward and economically underdeveloped country, entire families would leave as a matter of course, well into the twentieth century. My own mother was brought up in Westport, County Mayo in the 1930s. She, her four brothers and two sisters, her mother and father ended up in Britain.

It is very hard to measure this outpouring, but Akenson quotes some statistics that give some idea of its enormity. Between 1815 and 1870 a total of four to four and a half million people left Ireland. In 1890 nearly 40 per cent of Irish-born men and women (three million) were living abroad. When considering these figures it is important to bear in mind that roughly half of the emigrants were women – a massive proportion given emigration patterns elsewhere.

Emigration, then, is as Roy Foster says, 'perhaps the fundamental social fact of modern Irish history' (and not just modern history for, as we shall see, the phenomenon is as old as anything we know about Ireland). In a sense, emigration and the deeds of the emigrants can be seen as a parallel history of Ireland, an account of what Irishmen and women could do when circumstances allowed. For very often the stories of emigrants, as well as being the actions, important or otherwise, of individuals, have an Irish political dimension in which people emphasized they were acting as Irishmen or women. We see this in the military feats of the Wild Geese, exiled soldiers who fought for European Catholic armies in the seventeenth and eighteenth centuries, and who, although essentially mercenaries, regarded themselves as upholding Ireland's honour and acted as a beacon of hope to those they left behind clinging to the unrealistic belief they might return to liberate the old country by force of arms. It is equally apparent in the life of John F. Fitzgerald, the mayor of Boston and grandfather of JFK, whose life was dedicated to showing the Protestant establishment that Irish Catholics could be as good Americans as anyone else.

This desire to do well on behalf of Ireland, beyond its shores, is something we will encounter again and again, and is an eloquent testimony to the historic lack of opportunities for gifted and energetic Irishmen and women at home. The Irish emigrants had no core nation to belong to. For the Catholics, British rule meant they were to a certain extent exiles in their own land. Cultural disparagement of the Irish, as ugly, stupid and drunken, perpetuated in *Punch* cartoons of ape-like Paddies, created a strong desire in some to prove that the opposite was the case. Historians have been part of this process, so that some writings have striven too hard in the opposite direction to present a positive picture of Irish emigrants and to harp on achievement over failure. This is an underdog approach, unsurprising in the circumstances, but ultimately peculiarly condescending. Thus figures like Ned Kelly, the Australian bushranger, have been mythologized into rebels, animated at least partially by some incoherent sense of social justice.

Logic would suggest that the Irish are no better or worse than anyone else. Yet in popular cultural terms (notwithstanding the Victorian racists of *Punch*) they have often been presented in a remarkably favourable way. Even in Britain, Irishmen, as caricatures of what were meant to be national mannerisms and foibles, were staples of the music-hall stage in the late nineteenth century. Today, the Irish are arguably the most popular nation in Europe, an entity to which they have taken with avid enthusiasm and energy. Surprisingly, the IRA's actions have done little to damage the nation's image of sociability and co-operativeness.

Domestic service provided a start on the path of social advancement on arrival in the United States. For women like Katie, Hannah and Mary, pictured here in 1896, such work brought security and a degree of financial independence. Their remittances home helped pay the passages for succeeding waves of emigrants. Note the pride they take in the spotlessness of their Sunday best.

In America, after initial hostility, Irishness has almost always come to be portrayed positively, with affection, indeed admiration. On stage and TV and in popular songs (some of which were written by Jews) the Irish were presented as humorous, industrious and charming. Hollywood, when it dealt with the island's politics, invariably presented a simple picture of crude oppression – of stoical, rosy-cheeked colleens and their gallant but hopelessly outgunned menfolk on one side, and the cold, heartless British on the other. By Hollywood's standards, this perhaps represents something like accuracy. One of the compensations of victimhood – as the treatment of blacks by the movie industry shows – is that you can be assured of a sympathetic treatment on celluloid.

But were the Irish victims? To what extent has emigration been a curse and to what extent a blessing? Certainly the business of exile was painful, psychologically and physically. Revisionist attempts to retouch the big picture of emigration cannot alter the basic image of an epic exodus of the poor, driven out by hunger, discrimination and lack of opportunity. Those *en route* for the New World travelled in appalling, sometimes lethal, conditions (on some voyages to America, cholera wiped out half the passengers), and when they arrived they met with hostility and hardship.

As well as the material suffering there was terrible spiritual pain. It was, for almost all the emigrants to America, a one-way voyage, and they knew it. They would never go home again. Many tried to assuage the feeling of loss and loneliness in drink; many went mad.

Yet, if you were lucky, the rewards were substantial. And a heartening proportion of emigrants seem to have been lucky, or rather they made their luck (another strong feature of the big picture is that the resourceful, who had the wherewithal to travel, were the ones to take the great leap).

Irish judges and political barons at a New York City St Patrick's Day Parade. On the far right, with the beard, is the chieftain of the radical nationalist Clan na Gael organization, John Devoy.

In North America, in the age of westward expansion and at the birth of the era of muscular, aggressive capitalism, a victim could rapidly turn into a victor, and Irishmen and women were quick to seize the opportunities. The result is that the Catholic Irish in America have become a strong part of the ruling elite, starting with average socio-economic status at the turn of this century, crossing the median in the 1920s and forming a recognizably privileged group from the 1960s.

Data from the US National Opinion Research Center and the University of Michigan, relating to the 1960s and 1970s, revealed that the American ethnic group with the highest annual income is the Jews. Second are the Irish Catholics. The ethnic group with the highest average level of education is the Jews. Second are the Irish Catholics.

Those who might, historically, be seen as the enemies of the Irish Catholics have not done so well. Judged by income, people of Protestant Scottish and English ancestry come in the middle of the ethnic pack and third in terms of educational standing. The Catholic Irish have also outstripped the Irish Protestants, who, set against the same criteria, represent the least privileged white group.

One way of looking at these figures is to say that, in the parallel universe of the emigrant, the Catholic Irish have had their revenge on their economic and religious oppressors. Considering the story of Irish emigration it is hard not to keep falling into the same almost reflexive error. How many of us can say that when we hear the term 'Irish immigrant' we don't think immediately of a Catholic? But in America, where the influence of Irish arrivals has been the most profound, as Professor Akenson indicates, 'the bulk of the Irish ethnic group ... is and probably always has been, Protestant'. That is not the impression that has been given by Irish Catholic Americans, nor by the massive literature on the subject, nor in official celebrations of Irishness such as the New York St Patrick's Day Parade, which employs overwhelmingly 'Gaelic' imagery.

Making it. The McGovern family, children of immigrants from County Cavan, celebrating their success and prosperity in America in 1928.

Inevitably, the history of emigration has been turned into something of an ideological battleground on which the island's perpetual struggles can be refought. The experience of emigration frequently provides laboratory conditions in which great sociological theories can be tested, notably the question of the primacy of nurture or nature. Not that study of the Irish Empire could ever resolve such fundamental riddles. The incredible wealth and variety of the histories on offer mean that there are examples aplenty for every participant in the debate to back his or her case.

The story of immigration is as much about image as about fact. One of the singular things about the Irish Empire is that it is untrammelled by the practical burdens and constraints of a real state. Ireland abroad can present an image of how it sees itself and how it would like to be seen that is untarnished by contact with the realities of real power. It has no troublesome history in which Irish leaders wielded institutional power in a manner that contradicted its own view of its virtues and qualities.

One of the great 'what ifs' of history is to consider what might have been had Britain never colonized Ireland, had Ireland developed independently into an island state. What if its evolution had mirrored Britain's and it had become a maritime power, its fortunes built on overseas trade? Would there then have been a real Irish empire with colonies and Irish administrators bringing 'civilization' to the corners of the earth? And would these Irish imperialists have behaved any better than their British counterparts? Indeed, how would they have treated the British? Certainly, in America and Australia individuals showed themselves to be as harsh in their treatment of natives and as indifferent to indigenous land rights as any other white colonialist.

One prediction it is perhaps possible to make is that had such a thing come to pass it would have resulted still in a great outpouring of Irishmen and Irishwomen across the world, albeit this time in the role of conquerors. Ireland's fundamental wealth lies in its people. No matter how the state prospers it seems unlikely there will ever be sufficient opportunities in a land which, globalization notwithstanding, will always be at the edge of events to keep all its sons and daughters at home.

This is a book about those people, Catholic and Protestant, comfortable and destitute, male and female, who took their fate in their hands and set off on a journey which for most of them was a great leap into the unknown. For some of the émigrés, such as the MacMahon whose descendant Patrice was to become president of France or Patrick Kennedy of Wexford whose great-grandson John Fitzgerald Kennedy was to become president of the United States, the gamble could not have paid off more handsomely. For others, the venture ended in poverty, obscurity and homesickness.

Whatever the outcome, the millions who left Ireland's shores had something in common. They shared a conspicuous courage, and the poorer the emigrant the greater his or her bravery. Emigration is one of the great opportunities for heroism allowed to the poor. And the emigrants were heroes.

· I ·

A SEPARATE CULTURE

S EEN ON THE MAP, Ireland looks as an island should. Its ragged outline and the angle at which it lies in the sea give it the appearance of a mythological sea creature butting through the cold grey waters that seethe around it. Attempting to reach the island or trying to leave its protection would not be something to undertake lightly. The seas it swims in are not friendly. In ancient times, protected only by a frail vessel, you would have to be a resolute man to put out into them. Yet this is what the earliest inhabitants of the island may have done, possibly sailing to it at some point in the Mesolithic period of the Stone Age in tiny hide coracles from Scotland, landing on the coast of what is now Antrim. They lived at first as fishermen and food-gatherers, siting their homes near the water.

Later, in the Neolithic era (roughly 4,000 BC), they developed into farmers, cultivating the soil and raising domestic animals. They learned how to grind corn and bake bread and they cooked their food. They could make pots, spin and weave and were great builders, using large quantities of timber in the construction of houses, boats, causeways and defences. Eventually they turned to building in massive slabs of stones, not practical buildings but what were in effect mausoleums for the burial of their dead and temples to honour their gods.

These cairns and dolmens, standing stones and stone circles, still survive by the thousand, but little is known of the nature of the society that created them. Our ignorance begins to abate somewhat with the arrival of the Celtic colonists. The Celts first appeared in western Europe in about 600 BC, when they crossed the Rhine from the east. One group settled in what is now France and became the Gauls. Another tribe settled on the Iberian peninsula, which they used as a

(*Left*) One of the mysterious ancient monuments of Ireland. Drombeg stone circle, County Cork. (*Above*) The wild west coast.

A Neolithic passage grave site at Newgrange, County Meath.

base for sea voyages. It was these Celts who are thought to have predominated in the settlement of Ireland that began around 350 BC, with other Celts who had invaded Britain arriving periodically from the mainland.

The newcomers effectively superimposed themselves on the native tribes, borrowing and adapting much of what they found to augment their own language and practices. Thus Tara, the hill in County Meath where the high kings of Ireland were traditionally crowned, was a major cult site long before the Celts arrived. Similarly, as the historian Donnchadh Ó Corráin has pointed out, a lot of what has been been regarded as part of Celtic myth and cult, such as the sacred marriage of king and goddess and the linking of fertility to the reign of a good king, is in fact a much older inheritance from the original Neolithic agriculturalist inhabitants and their metal-using successors.

Whatever the ingredients that made up the cultural broth, something evolved on the island that was peculiarly Irish, with a language scholars call Goidelic, which differed from the Celtic spoken on the mainland. For the sake of convenience we can now begin to call these people Irish or Gaels to distinguish them from the other Celts who dominated the British archipelago.

What were these early Irishmen and women like? A highly coloured picture has come down to us through their own literature and the characterizations of later generations that continue to condition both Irish self-perceptions and the image of the Irish in the great world to this day. The writer Thomas Cahill has memorably described them as 'men and women, riding hard on horseback, drawing the blood of their enemies, leaping about in muscular dancing and passing the damp Irish night in vigorous coupling. Even their sorrows and deaths are tossed off with a shrug, though they understand tragedy and receive it as convulsively as any people.'

Prose epics like the *Tain Bo Cuailnge* ('The Cattle Raid of Cooley') which was first recorded in the eighth century and sets down an oral tradition that may go back to the beginning of the Christian era, provide a rich flavour of the court life of the times. It is a noisy world of drunken feasting and frank sexuality, of boasting and oath swearing. The heroine of one of the tales, Queen Medb, is to our eyes a thoroughly modern woman who regards herself as the equal if not the superior of her husband. The couple have a row about who has brought the greater wealth to the royal alliance. In a bid to trump her spouse she sends an emissary off to Cooley to ask the local chieftain Daire Mac Fiachna for the loan of his great brown bull to enrich the stock of her herd. As an inducement she offers 'a portion of the fine Plain of Ai equal to his own lands and a chariot worth thrice seven bondmaids and my own friendly thighs on top of that'.

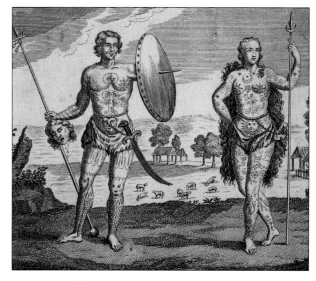

Such sauciness would have been considered shocking in later generations of Irishwomen. But in Medb we have a sharp portrait of a strong-minded, independent and proud woman who might be seen as a prototype of the hundreds of thousands of married and single women who centuries later would make the daunting trip from the homeland to an unknown destiny in America or Australia.

Celts in ancient Britain, as envisaged by what looks like a sixteenth- or seventeenth-century engraver. Their 'savagery' has been emphasized; and there is a strange contrast between the orderly scene in the background, set against the body decoration of the subjects and the severed head in the warrior's hand.

The Celts endured in isolation, untouched by the Roman occupation of the mainland, which began in earnest in AD 43 and lasted for the next 360 years, sending the Celtic societies of Britain into decline. Tacitus says that at one point during his campaign in southern Scotland, Agricola, the Roman governor of Britain in AD 77–84, looked across the strait at the Irish coast and mused about sending an expedition to conquer it. He 'saw that Ireland … conveniently situated for the ports of Gaul might prove a valuable acquisition'.

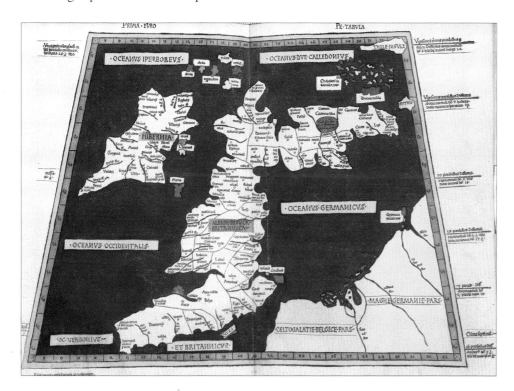

The British Isles showing Ireland according to Ptolemy's map of the second century AD.

Agricola was expressing an imperialist logic that would be acted upon centuries later with devastating consequences for the Gaels. But for the moment the Irish lived on, relatively untroubled by outsiders but frequently troubling each other in what seems to have been an almost structured existence of raid and reprisal.

We know quite a lot about the way life was ordered and lived and again, in the social arrangements of the times, we will find distant echoes of the manner in which the emigrants of later eras tackled life when faced with the challenge of a new land.

At one level there is much that is primitive and elemental about the Irish that stems largely from Celtic traditions. Like all the Celts they went naked into battle wearing only sandals and a gold necklace called a torc. They must have been a terrifying sight, howling like beasts, faces contorted in what they called the 'warp spasm', waving their swords and shields, driven on by the barbaric wailing of their pipers. The Romans had been shocked by them at first, but later were always respectful when they encountered them in battle.

Accounts of fighting contained in Irish heroic literature revel in the carnage and bloodshed. Warriors dressed their hair in lime and fought each other in chariots and in single combat and went head-hunting. One account of the doings of the champion Cuchulainn describes how he 'slew one hundred and thirty kings, as well as an uncountable horde of dogs and horses, women and boys and children and rabble of all kinds. Not one man in three escaped without his thighbone or his head or his eye being smashed, or without some blemish for the rest of his life.' It is interesting that dogs and horses come before women and children in the downward accounting of

Even in the imagination of the fairy-tale illustrator Arthur Rackham the ancient Irish were associated with tumult and disorder.

Cuchulainn's rampage. The story is of course full of wild exaggeration. But that is how the Irish liked it. Boasting was ritualized, and they seemed capable of being intoxicated by language, revering the bards and poets who celebrated and recorded life.

Yet beneath this exultant savagery there was a taste for order. Máire and Conor Cruise O'Brien wrote that 'the customary law of the Celtic peoples was highly developed and transmitted orally, apparently with extreme accuracy, from generation to generation by professional jurists. These were passionate casuists, conservatives and archaizers who, with the poets, historians and druids, as also smiths, artificers and musicians, formed part of the ... professional class.'

This legal code was known as the Brehon Law, a name stemming from *brithem*, the Irish word for judge, and it lasted, albeit modified by contact with Christianity, until the time of the Tudor campaigns against Irish chieftains of the second half of the sixteenth century, being finally abolished by the English in 1604. Under it, men belonged to a tribe and family and had no legal personality outside these units. Land and property were jointly owned and inherited.

The legal family was an extended kinship group known as the *derbfhine* or 'certain family' made up of the male descendants of a common great-grandfather. Wealth was reckoned in cattle. Outside the ranks of royalty and aristocracy, men of learning stood at the top of society and could move freely from clan to clan.

Law tracts in Latin and the vernacular from the eighth century, when Ireland had been Christianized, give a detailed picture of how, with a strong admixture of Church law, these practices evolved and of the shape they gave to society. There was a fairly strict but not unbreachable division of classes between kings, lords and commoners. The lord was distinguished from the commoner by his wealth and the fact that he had a number of clients bound to him by mutual responsibilities that were meant to result in mutual benefits.

The commoners were freemen, owning their own land and enjoying full rights in law. A law tract of the time describes the condition of an affluent example of the class, and his lot in comparison with his ancestors living on the same soil a thousand years later is an enviable one. He is said always to have two vessels in the house, one of milk and one of ale, two pigs and a plough. According to the season he has at home a sack of malt, a sack of salt for curing his butchered animals and a sack of charcoal for working iron. He has a corn kiln, a barn, a share in a mill to do his grinding, a dwelling house of twenty-seven feet, a lean-to of seventeen feet ... and so it goes on — twenty cows, two bulls, six oxen, twenty pigs. Below this class of man came the landless and at the bottom of the pile the hereditary serfs. Status was finely measured and the levels of compensation for outrage or injury awarded by the law were directly related to one's standing. As Donnchadh Ó Corráin observes, 'Kicking a bishop was a good deal more expensive than kicking a peasant ... and outraging a king was an offence for which few commoners could hope to be able to pay the compensation.'

In the client relationship between lord and commoner the lord inevitably came out the better. Clients were known as *cele* (companion) and there were two types. Free clients were often aristocratic themselves and bound themselves by formal homage to the lord's service, frequently making up part of his military retinue, accompanying him on cattle raids and sharing in the booty. Base clientship, on the other hand, resembled the arrangements of a medieval manor. Clients were advanced a grant of cattle or land in return for making certain payments back. In return the lord undertook to defend his client from outside aggression. Patrick McKenna, a scholar of Irish emigration to Argentina, has pointed out that something like this relationship was replicated by the Irish émigrés who fetched up on the pampas in the nineteenth century to raise sheep. Under it, the owner of a big flock would hand over a number of sheep for four years, during which time the immigrant would look after them and pay all expenses from his own pocket. At the end of it, owner and client would divide the flock.

A Celtic druid, part of the ordered face of ancient Irish society.

There has been a long-established tendency to look back on these days as a halcyon period and on the Brehon Law as a model of equitableness, preternaturally fair in the context of the times. But the client relationship could frequently be onerous, with a voracious lord able to make endless calls on a peasant's livestock and produce as well as demanding hospitality and labour services to build and to help out at harvest time. Later nationalist enthusiasts for the Brehon Law were reticent in their support for one aspect of the code. Inherent in it, as Queen Medb's conduct might suggest, is an easygoing attitude towards sex. Divorce was common and despite the efforts of the Church the upper classes, intent on ensuring the survival of the line, practised polygamy until the end of the Middle Ages.

Despite its orderliness this was an aggressive society that sought opportunities to expand. When considering the later history of Irish emigration it is important to remember that the first Irishmen to venture overseas went as raiders and colonizers. A great opportunity presented itself with the decline of Roman power in Britain in the fourth century. As the Roman grip on the province slackened, the Irish in the west and the Picts in the north sensed their chance. In 367 they launched simultaneous raids that ravaged Britain. With the virtual collapse of Roman rule at the start of the fifth century the way was open for a full-scale Irish settlement of Britain. Around this time colonizers from south-east Ireland established themselves in considerable numbers in south-west Wales in what is now Pembrokeshire, Carmarthenshire and Dyfed. A smaller settlement was made in north Wales in Anglesey, Carnarvonshire and Denbighshire. A third colony by Irish originating from County Cork was planted on the Cornish peninsula.

In his *Glossary*, Cormac, the scholar–bishop and King of Cashel, who died in 908, declares that 'the power of the Irish over the Britons was great and they had divided Britain between them into estates … and the Irish lived as much east of the sea as they did in Ireland and their dwellings and royal fortresses were made there'. This state of affairs, he said, was maintained 'for a long time, even after the coming of St Patrick to Ireland'. That is not much of a claim given that the saint's arrival is generally supposed to have happened some time in the first half of the fifth century, 432 being a popular date. Modern scholars are sure, though, that at some time in the late Roman period Irish colonists settled in south Wales, Cornwall and Devon and that a royal house was established in south Wales that lasted into the tenth century.

The most impressive of the Irish colonies on the mainland, however, was what became known as the kingdom of Dal Riata in Scotland. The name derives from the Dal Riata dynasty, which is placed by the Alexandrian Greek geographer Ptolemy, writing in the second century, in the extreme north-east of Ireland. When they began their overseas expansion is very unclear. Tradition, deemed by scholars to be unreliable, says it began in the third or fourth century. We do know that by the time St Columba made his mission from Ireland to the island of Iona off the west coast of Scotland in 563 the kingdom was expanding and by the middle of the ninth century united much of Scotland.

These colonial activities were a logical extension of the raiding that Irish war parties conducted up and down the west coast of Britain throughout the late Roman period, carrying off booty and, in particular, slaves. 'In the slavery business, no tribe was fiercer or more feared than the Irish,' notes Thomas Cahill. 'They were excellent sailors in skin-covered craft that they manoeuvred with consummate skill. Just before dawn a small war party would move its stealthy oval coracles into a little cove, approach an isolated farmhouse with silent strides, grab some sleeping children and be halfway back to Ireland before anyone knew what had happened.'

The raiding and the colonists' comings and goings across the Irish Sea, together with a certain amount of trading from the mainland to the island, meant that Ireland and the Irish received some exposure to the Roman world, but not enough to change significantly the fundamental character of their society. One manifestation of this is Ogham, the earliest form of written Irish, a system of strokes and dashes chiselled into the edges of standing stones, which is based on the Latin alphabet.

Some time in the early fifth century Irish slavers carried out a raid that was to result in a profound transformation of Irish society, though they can have had no idea of the consequences of their actions at the time. A large raiding party arrived on the west coast of Britain, probably by way of the Severn estuary, seized many young people and sailed them back to the slave markets of Ireland. Among them was a sixteen year old boy called Patricius.

From St Patrick's own writings, his *Confession* and his *Letter to the Soldiers of Coroticus*, we know a fair amount about his life and thought. The first is a spiritual biography and explanation of his mission, the second a tract of protest against the enslavement of some of his new converts. His date of birth remains a mystery, but

Standing stones still bear the markings of the Ogham writing system, as with this one found near a church at Kilmalkedar, Dingle peninsula.

we know that he was born in west Britain, the son of Calpurnius, a deacon and minor official who had a country estate. Patrick tells us that his grandfather Potitus had been a priest. He appears not to have been interested in a functionary's life. Whatever his plans, they were cut short by the arrival of the raiders. In Ireland he was sold as a shepherd slave and became the property of Miliucc, a local king who ruled in Antrim, and lived for six years a miserable life, 'chastened exceedingly and humbled in truth by hunger and nakedness and that daily'.

The six years' captivity seems to have effected a spiritual conversion. On his last night in slavery a voice told him in his sleep: 'Your hungers are rewarded: you are going home.' He woke up and the voice continued: 'Look, your ship is ready.' Patrick set off, not knowing where he was heading, and walked for 200 miles, possibly to a spot near modern Wexford, unchallenged by anyone despite his conspicuousness as a Briton, until he reached the sea, where sure enough a ship was waiting. The crew were loading a cargo of hounds for export to the continent. He approached the captain and offered to pay for his voyage (no explanation is given for the source of these funds) but was told 'You're wasting your time asking to sail with us.' Patrick turned away. 'I left them to go to the hut where I was staying, and on the way I began to pray and before I had finished my prayer I heard one of the sailors shouting after me: "Come quickly, they're calling you!" And right away I returned to them and they began to say to me: "Come on board, we'll take you on trust."'

(*Opposite*) St Patrick pictured visiting
a king, in a miniature taken from a
thirteenth-century manuscript.

The voyage to Europe took three days and when they arrived they encountered a scene of devastation. Thomas Cahill speculates that this might have been shortly after hundreds of thousands of Vandals, Alans and Sueves — starving after a population explosion had wiped out their food supplies — had thrown themselves across the frozen Rhine, sweeping aside the Roman legionaries waiting for them on the frontier of civilization and pouring into Gaul. The party could find no food. Men and dogs lay 'collapsed and half dead at the side of the road'. The captain began to taunt Patrick, saying 'How about it, Christian? You say your God is great and all-powerful, so why can't you pray for us? We're starving to death and there's little chance of our ever seeing a living soul.' Patrick replied: 'From the bottom of your heart, turn trustingly to the Lord my God, for nothing is impossible to him. And today he will send you food for your journey until you are filled, for he has abundance everywhere.' The sailors obediently lowered their heads in prayer and no sooner had they done so than they heard the drumming of hooves on the road and looking up saw a herd of pigs approaching.

It was several years before Patrick was to find his way home. There he was greeted with joy and wonderment by his parents, who must have supposed they had lost him for ever and who now begged him never to leave them again. But Patrick was restless. One night he had another vision, this time of a man called Victorius who was known to him in Ireland and who hands him a letter headed 'Vox Hibernicum' — The Voice of the Irish. Immediately he heard the noise of a great multitude crying 'We beg you to come and walk among us once more.' He was 'stabbed in the heart' by this visitation and woke up.

These visions increased until he could withstand them no more. After a dream in which he was told, 'He who gave his life for you, He it is who speaks within you,' he left home once more, this time for the continent. He travelled to a monastery, possibly that of Lerins on an island off the south of France, asked to train for the priesthood and was ordained and eventually sent on his way as a bishop–missionary back to the rainswept island that haunted him to begin his work of conversion.

It is worth retelling the story of Patrick because it contains many elements of the experience of emigration and exile. Irishmen, women and children, particularly the Catholics reared on tales of Ireland's greatest saint, must have derived comfort from his legend as they lay, hungry and seasick, in the stinking, heaving holds of ships bound for the unknown. Patrick's experiences reflect some of those of the average émigré. Exiles could take strength from the fact of his survival and eventual triumph and hope that their saga too would enjoy the same happy ending. To begin with, he is torn from his home against his will (no matter that he is going to, rather than from, Ireland), by force of arms rather than force of circumstances. He suffers great hardship and privation during his years of slavery. Yet by God's intervention he is redeemed and returns to his adopted homeland to finish his days in peace. It is a story full of sea voyages and brushes with danger in which the travellers are always ultimately under divine protection. This must have been a sustaining thought amid the perils and uncertainties of the emigrants' odyssey.

The Ireland that Patrick returned to was not an entirely pagan land. The first Christian missionaries began to arrive there in the late fourth and early fifth centuries,

ᵭᵉ ſᷓ́cᷓ̃ᵗᵒ pᷓᵗᵑᵒ ·ɪx·

Ⱥᵗᵑᵃᵘⁱᵗ ᵭᵘᵐ ſᵗᵒᵗʰ͛ᵓᵗᵖ
ᵗᵉᵍⁱ ᵗᵉ ᵭᵖⁱ pᵃſſⁱᵒᵑᵉ ᵱ
ᵭⁱᵗᵃ̃ᵗᵉᵗ· ſᵗᵃᵑſ ᵃᵑᵗᵉ ᵉᵘ
ᵗ ᵃᵱᵖᵒᵭⁱᵃ́ᵗⁱᵗ ſᵉ ſᵘᵖᵉᵗ ᵗᵉ
ᵗⁱᵗᵃᵐ qⁱᵐ ᵐᵃᵑᵘ ᵗᵉᵑᵉ
ᵇᵃᵗ ᵉᵗ ᵉᵃⁱⁱ ᵖᵉᵭⁱ ᵗᵉᵍⁱſ ⁱⁿ
pᵒſᵘᵉᵗᵃᵗ ᵃⁱ ᵃᵉᵘˡᵉᵒ ᵱᵗ

probably from Gaul, where the Church had been invigorated by the reorganization that followed the settlement of the Arian heresy at the council of Nicaea in 325, which held (among other beliefs) that God the Father and God the Son were separate beings. The island of Ireland fell within the notional authority of the Gaulish Church. The first hard date in the history of the Irish Church occurs in the chronicle of Prosper Tiro, an opponent of the heresy of the followers of the British monk Pelagius, who denied the doctrine of original sin. Under the year 431 he records that a certain Palladius, who may have been deacon at Auxerre, was sent as bishop to 'the Irish who believe in Christ'. The mission may have been connected to the activities of Germanus, who went to Britain to impose orthodoxy on the Pelagian heretics. Elsewhere Prosper records (undated) that Pope Celestine ordained a bishop for the Irish.

It is clear then that there was substantial Christian activity in Ireland before the patron saint's arrival, and there are glancing references in the seventh-century literature on his life to the British missionaries who predated him or were there when he arrived. Donnchadh Ó Corráin has written that 'Ireland is indebted overwhelmingly to Britain for its Christianity.'

The conversion of Ireland was to take some time, and 200 years after Patrick's arrival there was still evidence of a pagan rearguard action being fought. Nonetheless, the transformation seems to have been effected peacefully, for there is little record of martyrdom among the ranks of the missionaries. Christianity was attractive to the royal houses of Ireland and they seem to have recognized both its spiritual appeal and its political possibilities as a means of buttressing their temporal legitimacy and authority. By the ninth century the Church and the royal dynasties lived an intertwined life, in a mutually sustaining and supportive relationship. At this time some of the great monastic centres were the residences of provincial kings. The king of Leinster lived in the abbey of Kildare, where his brother was abbot and his sister abbess. Two or three of the

The ruins of the foundation at Clonmacnoise, one of the great centres of sixth-century monastic Ireland.

abbots of Emly were kings of Munster in the ninth century. As the five or six important provincial kings holding sway over Ulster, Munster, Leinster and Connaught gradually came to accept the notion of a paramount or high king, the Church's political position strengthened further.

Each element reinforced the authority of the other. Thus in Munster, Artri Mac Cathail, in return for receiving the imprimatur of the abbey of Emly and being ordained king in 793, allowed the abbey to levy a tax on the province. The churchmen in turn provided a theory for kingship and in doing so underpinned its legitimacy, drawing on the Old Testament to provide a biblical basis for the notion of an ordained and consecrated king. It is probable that the early medieval practice of consecrating kings as a ritual began with the Irish. At the same time they promoted kings as forces of control and order, urging obedience and giving their sanction to harsh punishments, including, frequently, death for those who broke the royal law.

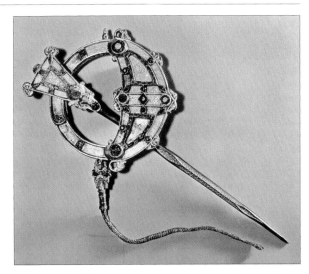

The quintessence of the Celtic aesthetic: the Tara Brooch, eighth century.

The organization of the Church, as it established itself in the sixth and seventh centuries, was essentially monastic. Through the new foundations, the written word was spread. As Máire and Conor Cruise O'Brien have noted, the introduction of writing ran counter to the preferences of the indigenous tradition, which was hostile to literacy as being destructive of memory and concentration and which remained remarkably resilient down the centuries, preserved in the practice of tale telling and the perpetuation of legends. A new language, Latin, came into use and at first the two traditions existed side by side in mutual dislike and distrust. Early on though, Irish scholars understood the need to adapt. But their first acts were to use the new language to record ancient laws — what the O'Briens see as a characteristic impulse to make 'innovation the servant of conservatism'.

Conservatism was found in all aspects of Irish society, perhaps a product of geographical insularity. Among the Church hierarchy there was a resistance to change, evidenced by their reluctance to adopt the new method for calculating Easter when it was imposed from Rome. However, it was not an ignorant rejection of all change. On the contrary. As the O'Briens observe, 'the ability to welcome what is new, to reconcile it with existing pieties and restate it in native terms is one of society's most marked characteristics, and we can still call the seventh and eighth centuries, with wonder and delighted recognition, Ireland's "Golden Age"'.

The big monasteries were able to maintain workshops which produced metalwork, calligraphy and illumination of a high order and there are many extant examples of the goldsmiths' and metalworkers' work such as chalices, bible covers and reliquaries to impress us with the standards of their craft. At the same time the monasteries were great centres of learning. Inside the Church a mandarin caste of scholars, grammarians, poets, lawyers and historians established itself. The tools of scholarship were clearly available. A text called *De Mirabilibus Sacrae Scripturae* ('Of the Wonders of Holy Scripture') written in 655 was able to draw on the works of a dozen fathers of the early Church. Other writings show that the Irish savants had a mass of material at their disposal. Thus, for a shining hour, Ireland, moored far out on the fringes of Europe, represented a beacon of learning and civilization in a darkened continent.

Shadowing and complementing Patrick in the history of the Christian efflorescence in Ireland is the gigantic figure of St Columba, known to the Irish by his monastic nickname of Colmcille, the 'Dove of the Church'. As with Patrick, we find in his life and work a link with the emigrant experience. We have a solid chronicler of Columba's life in the shape of Adamnan, himself a holy man who was abbot of the monastery of Iona a hundred years after its founder's time. Adamnan, who died in 704, was the greatest Irish churchman of his age and a friend of the rulers of Ireland and Northumbria. On the centenary of the death of Columba in 697 Adamnan held a synod of bishops, abbots and kings at which was promulgated an early attempt to legislate against the hideousness of war with a 'Law of the Innocents', which excluded women and children from battle and protected women from violence.

St Columba.

Columba was first named Crimthann or Fox, probably because he had red hair, and was high born enough to have been eligible for the kingship of Tara. He received a hybrid education, first being taught the bardic traditions of his ancestors before being turned over to Bishop Finian of Clonard to study in the discipline of Christianity. He was sent abroad to Gaul and visited the tomb of St Martin of Tours, founder of a monastic rule and, according to legend a sometime Roman soldier. The two traditions remained with him all his life. He became an energetic proselytizer and founder of monasteries, so that by the time he was forty-one years old he had established many religious houses, including the great foundations at Durrow and Kells. But it is also recorded that he remained friendly with the bards and poets, and he is presented in Irish song and prose as the champion and defender of poets and the old ways. On his death the chief poet of Ireland composed his eulogy.

He was a lover of beautiful objects, particularly illuminated books (the masterpiece of the genre, the Book of Kells, was produced in a Columban monastery), and a version of his life gives this addiction as the catalyst for his exile from his beloved Ireland. According to legend, as a student he fell in love with his master's psalter and decided to make his own secret copy by night. He had no candle but was able to see the text from the magical illumination of the five fingers of his left hand. He was discovered and brought before the local king, Diarmait, who forced him to return the copy. Columba felt humiliated and when, some time later, Diarmait ordered one of his monks to be killed, Columba had his revenge. Calling on his royal kinsmen he launched an attack on Diarmait and his forces, beating them soundly and suffering only one casualty in the process. But subsequently Columba was excommunicated for the sin of taking up arms and sent into exile. He set off in 563 with twelve companions, sailing north until they came to the island of Iona off the west coast of Scotland, where he founded his most famous monastery. It was a simple, spartan place. Each monk had his own hut, and there was a refectory, a kitchen, a scriptorium, a library, a kiln, a smithy, a mill, barns and a small church. The island became a place of pilgrimage for visitors from all over the archipelago. As numbers expanded Columba sent off groups of monks, twelve at a time, to found new monasteries.

Columba's disappearance from Ireland's shores and his acceptance of a life of isolation far from the privileges he had known as a noble and a leading prelate was part of what the O'Briens term an 'extraordinary Irish manifestation' of the times, that is the movement of the 'Exiles for Christ'. 'The essence of this exile' they explain, 'was a bloodless or "white" martyrdom, a kind of civil death. A man left his tribe, not only severing the links of natural affection but abandoning everything that had constituted his secular identity, and sought some desert place where, living in austerity and prayer, he might once again be born again of Christ.'

It is possible to see in this monastic tradition a spiritual ancestor of the emigrant experience of exile. Of course there are fundamental differences in the two circumstances. The monks were entering painfully but in the end willingly into anchorite seclusion or into the tiny world of the island foundation, and by and large the men and women who took part in the great nineteenth-century emptyings of Ireland were responding to economic imperatives. But both in their way were seeking in exile a better life, and ultimately redemption. It is not too fanciful to say that the monks of the Columban tradition left something in the folk memory of the Irish race that made emigration and exile a not totally alien, and therefore perhaps a slightly more easily borne, ordeal.

By the end of the eighth century, Ireland's Golden Age was drawing to an end. It had been free from invasion since prehistoric times and its calm had been disturbed only by the endless power-struggle between the competing royal houses. None of the aspirations to high kingship had been realized. But the country was otherwise remarkably cohesive, and officialdom and the Church strove to create a sense of unity. Scholars pretended to find that all the competing tribes were descended from a single set of ancestors, and lawyers spoke of the codes of practice of the 'island of Ireland'.

Ireland's relative tranquillity, its ecclesiastical riches and its agricultural wealth made it a magnet for the seafaring barbarians of the north. Viking innovations in boat design meant that Ireland fell within easy reach of the Norsemen's longships. In the 790s they seemed to be everywhere in the British isles, arriving out of the sea, looting, raping and burning, then disappearing again. The monasteries were obvious targets. Iona was attacked first in 795, again in 802 and again in 806, when the Vikings killed sixty-eight members of the community.

By the 830s the raids had become bigger and more prolonged and the Vikings started to use the big rivers, the Shannon, the Boyne, the Liffey and the Erne, to penetrate to the centre of the island. They began to settle, particularly in Dublin (which grew into a major trading centre and one of the richest cities in Europe), Limerick and Waterford. The Vikings killed many and wrought havoc wherever they went. But Irish society and especially the monastic infrastructure proved remarkably resilient in resisting them. The Irish kings rallied against them and managed to inflict a number of significant defeats. The Norsemen, or Ostmen as they called

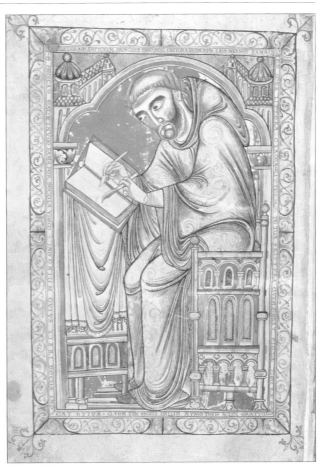

Monasteries provided both a seat of great learning and workshops for creating beautiful artefacts.

themselves, never succeeded in taking over whole kingdoms, as their counterparts did in England, where they established dominion over half the country and settled intensively. In some respects they can be seen as a positive force. Their marine technology caught on in the areas they raided, and northern kings built up their own navies. The Ostmen themselves developed trade, taking over the traffic in slaves and introducing the silver and gold from their profits into the currency. Eventually they became drawn into the ever shifting pattern of alliances and wars by which the Irish kings attempted to establish their authority over the island.

Towards the end of the tenth century, one man emerged who would, for a while, succeed in making himself undisputed high king of Ireland. Brian Boru was of the relatively obscure Dal Cais dynasty, kings of north Munster. After his brother was assassinated he succeeded him and revenged himself on the Ostmen of Limerick who had killed him before turning towards what was sure to be the greatest obstacle to his ambitions – the Ui Neill dynasty, whose members claimed the kingship of Tara and by extension paramountcy in the island. After inconclusive campaigning, Brian and the Ui Neill ruler Mael Sechnaill II divided the country between them.

(*Opposite*) A page from the exquisitely illuminated Book of Kells.

An enduring symbol of Irishness. The High Cross at Kells, County Meath, photographed in the late nineteenth century.

Later Brian allied himself with the Ostmen of Dublin, sought the blessing of the Church and succeeded in undermining the Ui Neill to the point where he was able to style himself 'Emperor of the Irish'.

His triumph did not last long. How could it have done in the institutionally fractious power structures of the times? The absence of a hereditary tradition in the high kingship meant that authority had to be constantly asserted, ensuring that the country was always echoing with the clash of arms. Brian was killed at the battle of Clontarf on Good Friday 1014, fighting a force of Ostmen and the soldiers of the perpetually rebellious kingdom of Leinster. It was nonetheless counted a victory.

Brian's rule, from 975 to 1014, is seen as a period of recovery after the devastation caused by the Ostmen. He consciously tried to build island-wide institutions, notably by establishing Armagh, the seat of St Patrick, as having ecclesiastical primacy in Ireland. After his death, no one was to succeed in bringing the various provincial dynasties under the control of one clan. The result was an endless jostling for position that failed to produce any decisive result.

The lack of any political evolution was compounded by a decline in the vigour and moral authority of the Church. Increasingly the abbots of the great foundations were laymen and their authority grew at the expense of the bishops. Indeed lay

A stone carving from Gotland depicting the Viking raids.

power was to be seen everywhere, and this power was increasingly abused. The clergy's conduct seems to have worsened too and there were reports of the sale of indulgences and sexual misconduct. At the same time, the old fashioned structures of the Church became the object of disapproving scrutiny by continental and British reformers, especially the Gregorians, who were transforming the organization of the Church in Europe.

The business of reform was eventually tackled at three national synods at Cashel in 1101, Rath Breasail in 1111 and Kells-Mellifont in 1152. These imposed a diocesan system on the Irish Church and confirmed the primacy of Armagh. One major consequence of the reforms was that monasteries were now separated from dioceses. The result is that the former were gradually taken over by foreign, reforming orders, notably the Cistercians. The newcomers were tough on abuses, abolishing the hereditary succession of abbots and insisting on the rule of celibacy. There was a certain amount of resistance to the new strictness. But while the reforms may have been a victory for orthodoxy the results have been judged by some scholars to have been disastrous for the monastic culture that had so enriched Ireland since the coming of Christianity. In Ó Corráin's words, 'the bishops took over much monastic land and, in time, formerly powerful monasteries were to sink to the level of parish churches … The reformers destroyed the social, economic and cultural base of Irish learning. Nothing replaced the greater monasteries with their schools and learned cadres, now robbed of their resources and their status.'

The monastic scholars moved out and joined with another displaced group, the praise poets employed to laud the achievements and history of royal houses, who lingered on from pre-Christian culture. Clerical lawyers became secularized and by the thirteenth century even the Irish script that had swirled so magnificently over the manuscripts and law tracts and documents of the Golden Age had all but disappeared.

The stage was now set for the appearance of a much greater threat to the unique culture that had grown up in Ireland in the Christian era. Its arrival was unheralded, one of those accidents of history, all the more dramatic and profound in its effects for being unforeseen. It emerged from the vagaries of the dynastic struggles that continued on the island through the eleventh and twelfth centuries. After Brian Boru, Mael Sechnaill II had established himself as high king, but after his death in 1022 no one was able to make a successful claim to the vacant throne, if thus it can be described. The power vacuum determined that the military campaigning dragged on, and kings spent months in the field, turning over the governance of their lands to officials, and the increasing use of cavalry and naval forces complicated and increased the cost of war. Inevitably, it was the royal subjects who paid for the maintenance of the armies, in obligations and taxes. The chroniclers presented this world with the expected courtly gloss, a tableau of chivalry, beauty and honour. The realities of twelfth-century political life with its endless wars and treacherously shifting alliances could hardly be more different from the literary version.

A lascivious monk being spied on. It was this kind of misconduct which, by the eleventh and twelfth centuries, led to the moral authority of the Church being questioned.

The great reformer St Bernard of Clairvaux in Cistercian habit, taming the devil, pictured in the sixteenth-century *Flemish Book of Hours*.

By the middle of the twelfth century another dynamic figure who seemed to have the energy, military skills and determination to pull off the great feat of uniting Ireland under his rule appeared on the scene. He was Turlough O Connor, king of Connaught, the greatest warrior of the century. He built castles and strategic bridges across the Shannon and maintained a sizeable army and navy. After destroying the power of the Munster kings in a series of campaigns over fifteen years he set about realizing his ambition. After his death in 1156 supreme power was assumed by the Ui Neill king Muirchertach MacLochlainn. He in turn allied himself with Dermot MacMurrough, king of Leinster. They in turn were opposed by Rory O'Connor, the new king of Connaught. In 1166, after a prolonged struggle to retain control of Dublin, now recognized by the Irish kings as the strategic keystone to the island, MacLochlainn and MacMurrough were defeated and driven out by O'Connor, who banished MacMurrough to England — a fatal move for him as it was to turn out. Once in England Dermot appealed for help to the Plantagenet ruler, Henry II, who was king of England as well as lord of the Angevin areas of France. The request coincided with Henry's own tentative plans. Like Agricola in the first century AD, others had seen the strategic and political benefits of occupying Ireland. The idea of invasion had been discussed at the courts of William the Conqueror and Henry I. It had surfaced again at the start of Henry II's reign, apparently at the instigation of the Archbishop of Canterbury, who was angry at having lost metropolitan rights over the see of Dublin in 1152, when it opted to become an Irish archbishopric. The archbishop dispatched his secretary to Rome for an audience with Adrian IV, the only Englishman ever to have become pope. Adrian was concerned by the moral condition of the Irish Church and saw an opportunity for reform. He obliged with a bull of legitimation, investing Henry and his successors with the right to rule Ireland, accompanying it with a gold and emerald ring to commemorate the grant.

Henry had his own reasons for invading. He wanted land for his own sons and territory too with which to satisfy the greed and ambitions of his more truculent vassals. His own grip on power in England was not secure, however, and so when Dermot first approached him he chose not to get actively involved. Instead, in return for his fealty Dermot was given permission to recruit among the king's more adventurous subjects. He found them mainly among the lords whose fiefdoms marched with the Welsh border.

Until now the successive invaders and conquerors of the British mainland had mostly stayed away from Ireland. There had been trading and raiding contacts with the Romans, and a certain amount of fraternization and commerce with the Anglo-Normans. By and large, though, on the temporal front and leaving aside the religious fertilization of the island, foreign politics and outside influences such as the arrival of the Norsemen had been absorbed and adapted into Irish society. Now this was all to change. The realities of power and economics would inevitably have meant that Ireland would have been drawn into the feudal embrace of the Anglo Normans. But that process was now taking place with a brutal suddenness that would change the nature of society and establish a relationship with the bigger island that would effectively determine the course of Irish history almost to the present day. A system was superimposed that henceforth bound Ireland's affairs tightly to those of England, effectively ending centuries of independence and subordinating the interests of the native inhabitants to those of the dominant party in the arrangement. Ireland was a resource to be exploited economically and politically and otherwise neglected, unless local unrest attracted the reluctant attention of the crown. The poverty, insecurity and lack of opportunity that were ultimately to ensue from the relationship were the forces that were to turn the Irish into one of the great émigré nations of the world. At the time, however, the arrival of the Normans was probably seen by the local chieftains as a development they could turn to their advantage.

Reverse of the royal seal of Henry II, 1133–1189.

·2·

ENGLISH INVASION

THE NORMAN KNIGHTS whom Dermot MacMurrough brought back with him to Ireland in 1169 were adventurers, less interested in acting as agents of Leinster's king than in pursuing their own considerable dreams of acquiring land, power and wealth. Foremost among them was Richard de Clare, better known as 'Strongbow'. MacMurrough was lavish in his promises of land and dynastic marriages and there seems to have been no shortage of Norman barons who saw the expedition as a great opportunity. Between 1169 and 1171 they reconquered MacMurrough's lands for him and even took Dublin. After Dermot's death in May 1171 Strongbow crushed a revolt of the Leinster Irish and established himself as lord of the province. These suc-

cesses alarmed King Henry, who set off in October of the same year to establish his authority. But, even before he reached Ireland, Strongbow had intercepted him, assuring him of his loyalty, and was rewarded with the formal grant of Leinster. During his progress from Waterford to Dublin the English king received numerous pledges of loyalty from many of the native kings, and from the Ostmen of Wexford.

Thus the first English king came to Ireland. Already it must have seemed to Henry that he had acquired an asset and a liability. Ireland had land in an era when land was the foundation of life and power. However, the land was not his; nor did it even belong to the likes of Dermot MacMurrough, who by Irish custom were holding it on behalf of their tribe. Force of arms could settle that problem – when Henry could turn away from his other concerns and when the resources were available. But beyond that was the question of maintaining authority. It was clear from the outset that this would be a difficult business. Not only was there a

(*Left*) Dermot MacMurrough, Irish king of Leinster, arrives in England to seek the help of the Normans, pictured in a late fourteenth-century manuscript. (*Above*) King Henry and his men reach the Irish coast in 1169. (From a fifteenth-century chronicle)

A bard and harpist entertain an Irish chieftain at an alfresco feast.

wide sea between the two lands. There seemed to be a spirit of independence inherent in the air and soil of the place that might well be infectious.

In the encounter between the Irish and the Normans an old world was meeting a new one. The Irish were different, there was no doubt about that. The language they spoke, the food they ate, their manner of thinking were archaic. The aristocracy lived what was already recognizably an esoteric way of life by European standards. A Gael lord dined out of doors on barely cooked meat and salads and yogurt, living on the move, disdained armour as 'ungentlemanly', and, psychologically restricted to consideration of his own immediate interests and concerns, was preoccupied with preserving and expanding them.

A people like this lacked the cultural wherewithal to deal with the depredations of an aggressive, innovative power. Their best hope lay in absorption rather than outright opposition. And this, to some extent, is what happened. The newcomers intermarried with Irishwomen and became part of the complex warp and weft of tribal alliances, learning the Irish language, and adopting local dress and customs with such enthusiasm that as contemporaries observed they became *hiberniores hibernis ipsos*, more Irish than the Irish themselves. Many of the early settlers' names are preserved in contemporary Irish nomenclature – Joyce (De Jorz), Burke (De Burgo), Fitzgerald and so forth.

Nonetheless the Old English – as the descendants of the Norman colonists are known in order to distinguish them from the post-Reformation arrivals – maintained a contemporary perception of how power was structured and a keen appreciation of their rights in relation to those of their nominal sovereign. The English kings needed them, and in the mid-fourteenth century three great earldoms of Desmond (Fitzgerald), Ormond (Butler) and Kildare (Fitzgerald) were created in an attempt to strengthen the crown against the native Irish. The Norman lords had their own ambitions, however. Exploiting the geographical advantage of their island position the leading nobles gradually asserted their own authority at the expense of the crown's, so that its sway diminished to the point where it was focused on a small area around Dublin, enclosed by an earthenwork rampart known as the Pale. In the second half of the fifteenth and the first half of the sixteenth century the Fitzgeralds of the House of Kildare in particular established themselves in semi-regal style, in direct defiance of the English monarchy.

In the fourteenth and fifteenth centuries the Hundred Years War and the Wars of the Roses had kept the English kings too occupied to spare the time or resources needed to exert control over Ireland. With Henry VIII that changed. When in 1534 Lord Offaly, son of the ninth Earl of Kildare, declared that Henry's break with Rome made him a heretic and declared himself the champion of the Pope, the reaction was swift and terrible. The lands of the Fitzgerald family were confiscated, and Offaly and his five uncles were brought to London and put to death at Tyburn. With the power of the house of Kildare smashed, Henry in 1541 had himself declared in Dublin 'King of this land of Ireland as united, annexed and knit for ever to the Imperial Crown of the Realm of England'. As frequently in the past, the Gaelic lords went along with English assertions of sovereignty. At the ceremony the proclamation was read out to them and they replied by giving their 'liberal assents'. As the historian Robert Kee explains, 'The Gaelic chiefs ... had no scruples about submitting to the authority of an English king when this proved tactically necessary. Their one concern was to be left free to pursue their private interests and ambitions by their subtle system of tribal alliances, and to look after their lands with the minimum of outside interference.'

Richard II (1367–1400) dining with his English and Anglo-Irish nobles. Although they did not renounce their nominal sovereign, in effect, the Irish nobility succeeded in ruling Ireland throughout the fourteenth and fifteenth centuries.

The alacrity and comprehensiveness with which the Irish aristocracy, Old English and Gaelic, at first accepted Henry's claim suggest that they were aware that a great change was afoot and it was better to place themselves smartly on the winning side. The earls of Tyrone, Desmond and Thomond, Gaelic chiefs such as the Fitzpatrick, O'Connor, O'Murphy and O'Carrol, wrote to the king calling on God to witness that 'we acknowledge no other King on earth except your majesty'.

These expressions of loyalty could not satisfy the desire of the Tudor state to establish its power in Ireland. And power was to be applied through the instruments of land and religion, the two most explosive elements in Ireland's history. At first the Tudors moved carefully, preferring persuasion to force. A system of 'surrender and regrant' was introduced whereby lords would hand over the title of their lands to have it regranted to them but on feudal terms. Many went along with it. But the innovation clashed directly with existing legal concepts of land ownership. For lesser lords, the land that their overlords was surrendering to the king was not theirs to give. Where resistance was encountered, the authorities resorted to confiscation. When protests broke out in 1557 they were put down with a brutality which, the Protestant historian W.E.H. Lecky declares, 'has seldom been exceeded in the pages of history'.

An approving allegory of Henry VIII's rejection of the authority of Pope Clement VII.

The issue of religion was less immediately contentious. Nonetheless, the loyalty of the ruling class to the notion of papal spiritual authority was considerably deeper than that of the mainland aristocracy. The clergy, in what must count as one of the most successful defences ever mounted in the war of ideas, encouraged the ruling class to stay firm. They advised the nobility to draw a distinction between spiritual and temporal allegiance to the crown. Thus, those who refused to accept the spiritual authority of the crown and declined attendance at the state church could still attempt to maintain their political loyalty, though this position became increasingly difficult to hold to as time passed. The launching of the counter Reformation, aimed at throwing back the forces of Protestantism, in the middle of the sixteenth century forced Catholic lords to choose between their sovereign and their religion and to place an unbearable strain on their allegiance. But adherence to the old religion was to remain remarkably firm among both the Old English and the Gaelic nobility, as well as among the population at large, ensuring that there was a strong Catholic community embracing all classes to greet the accession to the English throne of the Catholic James II in 1685.

Throughout the sixteenth century the colonization of Ireland had continued. The Pale around Dublin was fortified with garrisons. Military 'plantations' were established in the midlands by the Catholic monarch, Mary. The Irish problem was of little interest to Elizabeth when she came to the throne in 1558, but she was persuaded quickly of the strategic necessity of dealing with it. The crown's relative weakness in Ireland and the power of the Church meant that the Reformation had failed to take hold there, a fact that was to ensure the continuing fractiousness of relations between the two islands. The persecution that ensued in an attempt to eradicate spiritual loyalties guaranteed that large elements of the population from the aristocracy to the peasantry were alienated, insecure and always ready for rebellion. Floating menacingly at England's back it presented a great opportunity for the foreign enemies of the English and the enemies of the Reformation.

The Irish lords, meanwhile, were encouraged by England's enemies to believe that they could expect support in the event of an uprising. Shane O'Neill of Ulster was the first to rebel, but the Spanish and French help he was promised never came and the revolt petered out with his death in 1567. There were further rebellions in Munster under James FitzMaurice FitzGerald, who sought help from France and Austria. There was a third uprising led by the Earl of Desmond in Leinster and Munster which lasted from 1579 until he was killed in 1583. We have some idea of the nature of the warfare from an eyewitness description by the Elizabethan poet and thoroughly modern Tudor Edmund Spenser, who recounted the misery caused by the crushing of the Desmond rebellion: 'Out of every corner of the woods and glens they came creeping forth upon their hands, for their legs would not bear them; they looked like anatomies of death; they spoke like ghosts crying out of their graves; they did eat the dead carrions, happy where they could find them; yea and one another soon after, insomuch as the very carcases they spared not to scrape out of their graves.'

Elizabeth I. The Irish rebelled against her efforts to impose the Reformation more rigorously on Ireland.

The rebel Shane O'Neill submitting to Sir Henry Sidney, Lord Deputy of Ireland, in 1566, as imagined by contemporary engraver John Derricke.

This sight provoked disgust rather than pity. Unlike the Normans, the Tudor colonizers were impervious to Ireland's magic. Spenser reacted to all around him with a fastidious horror. When the Irish burned down his house he furiously considered a Hitlerian punishment for their unruly ways: 'Should the Irish have been quite rooted out? That were too bloody a course, and yet their continual rebellious deeds deserve little better.'

With each failed rebellion came confiscation and plantation by Englishmen. The Desmond lands were handed over to a syndicate of which Sir Walter Raleigh was the head. Often the plantations failed to take root. Surrounded by strange people speaking a strange language, the settlers became demoralized and departed, enabling the dispossessed to move back in, though this time without any legal title to their old lands, ancient or modern. As Robert Kee notes, it was 'this lack of any right to be on the land on any other terms than those of mere sufferance, in contrast with a certain post-feudal mutual obligation which characterised relations between landlord and occupier elsewhere in Europe, that was to determine the condition of the Irish peasant for three centuries'.

The last rebellion of the period was that of Hugh O'Neill, Earl of Tyrone. With its failure and his departure in 1607 we can be said to be entering the first properly identifiable phase of the history of Irish emigration. O'Neill had been brought up in London as an Elizabethan gentleman but entered easily into the swirling world of ever changing loyalties that were a feature of the Irish aristocracy's attempts to maintain its interests when confronted with the Tudor political and military machine. In 1595 he joined forces with Red Hugh O'Donnell and rebelled, at the same time seeking support from Spain. The rebels had one substantial victory against the government forces in Ulster at the Yellow Ford in 1598. The revolt spread southwards and Elizabeth's commander, the Earl of Essex, was forced to seek a truce. His replacement, Mountjoy, proved more energetic. The Spanish sent a force of 4,000 to reinforce O'Neill but not enough to make a difference. At Kinsale on Christmas Day 1601 the rebels were defeated. O'Donnell fled to Spain. O'Neill surrendered, submitted, was pardoned and stayed on. But diminished, with no hope of regaining his position and in permanent fear of his life there was nothing to keep him in Ireland. On 14 September 1607, together with the Earl of Tyrconnell (the brother of Red Hugh), he set sail from Lough Swilly and Ireland, never to return.

The Flight of the Earls, as it became known, remains a hugely emotional and symbolic event in Irish history. O'Neill's final voyage is seen as a farewell, in the dimming twilight, to the rule of the Gaels in Ireland. In fact the Gaelic aristocracy were to linger on for some time longer. O'Neill's — essentially voluntary — departure set two very important trends in motion that are vital to our story. First, it opened the way for the wholesale plantation of Ulster by Protestants. Second, it established a tradition of exile among the old Irish upper classes who might have been hoped to provide some sort of bulwark against English rule for the great mass of people who ultimately bore the brunt of the English occupation and colonization.

But it is the first consequence that was immediately apparent. The earls left behind vast estates in six of the nine counties of Leinster. On this confiscated land were planted English settlers, all of them Protestant. With the arrival of the new colonists a further gap opened up in Irish society. The old division between Gael and Norman, at the higher levels of society at least, had long been blurred by intermarriage and the merging of cultures. Political differences had been determined by attitudes towards overseas authority. Now a new distinction was emerging, that of religion. This was to set the course of the social and political development of Ireland in the modern age.

The death of the fifteenth Earl of Desmond in 1583.

Hugh O'Neill, Earl of Tyrone, seeks a truce with the Lord Lieutenant at Kinsale, 1601.

Dolose agunt filij iniquitatis

·3·
THE PROTESTANT ASCENDANCY

THE FLIGHT OF THE EARLS has taken on an aura of romantic finality. But, like all reluctant exiles, as they stood watching the coastline of Ireland dim and fade on the horizon the Ulster chieftains cannot have supposed the separation from their homeland would be permanent. Their intention was to continue the search for help overseas among their natural allies and England's political and religious enemies, the powers of Catholic Europe. Recent research has shown that O'Neill in particular was successful at establishing himself at the Spanish and papal courts, and the earls' retinues formed a distinct military force with their own chaplains based in Spanish Flanders. Their ultimate aim was always the liberation of their homeland. A 'Memorial of Hugh O'Neill to the King of Spain' in 1610 requests King Philip to 'send an army secretly and in the name of his holiness to Ireland'. In the end the earls' efforts were fruitless. But the politico-religious circumstances of the times were conducive to hope, and O'Neill was still actively pursuing his ambitions when he died in Rome in 1616.

The earls and their successors, and the Catholic soldiers later known as the Wild Geese who followed them into exile at the end of the seventeenth century, are seen as establishing the tradition of Irish overseas soldiering. In fact the pattern was already evident. Irish soldiers of fortune had started going to Europe in the thirteenth century. Unlike the Wild Geese they often fought on behalf of the English, and there is a record of Irish soldiers serving with the English forces against the Welsh in 1243. Irish troops fought on the winning side in the Wars of the Roses and helped suppress the rebellions of Lambert Simnel and Perkin Warbeck. Depictions of the battle of Crécy (1346) show Irish formations

(*Left*) Irish soldiers fought for English kings as early as the Battle of Crécy in the fourteenth century, but were also objects of fun, being mocked in this cartoon (*above*) for preferring to 'eate than fight'.

Irish men-at-arms, 1631, in the service of the Swedish monarch Gustavus Adolphus during the Thirty Years War.

under the command of the Black Prince, and it is probable that there were Irish at Agincourt. In *Henry V*, Shakespeare places an Irishman, Captain McMaurice, at the battle, which suggests that such a figure would have been if not commonplace then at least not unusual at the time. Irish soldiers and their chieftains, the remnants of the defeated forces of the Earl of Desmond, sought refuge in Spain in the mid 1580s and Irish exiles aided the preparation of the Spanish Armada which set sail in 1588 in the hope that its success would lead to the restoration of their lands and religion. Some of them served as sailors and guides with the fleet.

With the departure of the earls and, later, the flight of the Wild Geese their mercenary motives are gilded by a political and religious purpose which has ensured them a prominent place in Irish myth. We will return to the romantic figure of the itinerant Irish swordsman, his chivalry and good humour underlaid with the melancholy of exile, that features in so much sentimental Irish literature. Under-represented, indeed invisible in ballad and poem, though, are the lowlier victims of war we find among the Irish wanderers who travelled from parish to parish through England in the same period as the Tudors were setting the seal on their domination of Ireland.

The researches of the historian Patrick Fitzgerald into the poor Irish migrants to England in the period 1560–1640 show Irish names cropping up frequently in parish records of the period kept by churchwardens dispensing relief to the worthy poor. They also appear in the documents relating to the arrest and examination of vagrants, and they are specifically referred to in a statute of 1572 which states that they should be punished and returned to Ireland. Irish beggars appear in Scotland too, to the intense annoyance of the authorities, leading the Scottish Privy Council in 1629 to issue a proclamation ordering the removal of 'great nombers of strong and sturdie Yrish beggars … wandering the country in troops extorting alms'. The reputation of the vagrants was low, and consorting with them was in itself an offence. In 1602 the

Church authorities of Dundonald in Ayrshire summoned before them a number of parishioners accused of entertaining and harbouring a certain John Burg (Burke) described as a 'maisterful beggar' and 'Yrland man' who was accompanied by a harlot.

The volume of emigrants to England and Scotland was sufficient to sustain a marine trade. Among those practising it was Maurice Keysons, alias Curry, who was arrested in 1630 after disembarking a sizeable number of migrants on the Somerset coast. Examined by the justices his servant William Welsh explained that his master rationalized his activities by saying that 'as long as there were English in Ireland he would bring Irishmen into England for if Englishmen would depart from Ireland the Irish had no need to come into England'. Welsh ended up with Keysons in the stocks.

It would appear that the arrivals created alarm not because the population had never seen an Irish person before but because of their numbers and their destitute and ragged condition, which seemed to signify to the Tudor English mind a threat to order. Yet the Irish were already well represented among the servant class where their qualities were highly regarded. A pamphlet of 1599 advocating that Englishmen should colonize Ireland and simultaneously exhorting employers to import Irish labour speaks of Irish servants, once detached from their priests, as being 'very faithful and loving' and commends those already working in England as 'industrious and commonly our best gardeners, fruiters and keepers of horses'. Irish grooms appear as characters in a number of Jacobean dramas.

These somewhat condescendingly admired, one might almost say tame, Irish folk were not what concerned the authorities. In parallel with the image of the cheery, efficient good-natured servant who well understood his place, another stereotype took root. The two species were to establish themselves in the social iconography of the main host countries where the Irish were to set foot. Whereas the first could be taken

An Irish servant and his master, as seen by engraver John Derricke, 1581.

as a paradigm of lower class docility, the second was regarded as an enemy of order and, in the semi-paranoid psychology of Tudor and Jacobean authority, a considerable political threat. We catch a glimpse of these Irish in a report by William Waad, lieutenant at the Tower of the London, to the Earl of Salisbury in which he describes in the authentic, wrinkle-nosed tones of contemporary English officialdom a 'new built

The killing of Protestant settlers during the Ulster rebellion of 1641.

land called Hoge's Lane' in the east of the city where he had discovered 'a cluster of base tenements, termed Knockfergus, peopled with Irish of very base sort'. Waad claimed that from their tenements, laden down with illegitimate children, they ventured out during the day bothering decent citizens with their begging and petty crime. Elsewhere in a report to the Lord Mayor of London in 1593, the Privy Council spoke of the 'great numbers of poor Irish people … begging in and about the city'.

What drove these people out? It seems clear that many of them were the victims of the rebellions and wars that wracked Ireland during the sixteenth and seventeenth centuries and can be counted as much casualties of the great changes as their nostalgically commemorated social superiors. In so far as we can get any picture of them, most would appear to be youngish, between fifteen and forty-five, with the majority of those being under thirty. They came, fundamentally, because they were hungry. The destruction of war, the loss of agricultural production that the prosecution of it entailed and a run of bad harvests meant that for those outside the towns emigration was a survival stategy. The English authorities recognized as much. By the end of 1587 the government tried to stop the exodus by ordering the town of Munster to take back deportees and advised the lord deputy of Ireland to ensure that no one else was allowed to embark. Bristol employed a special beadle to turn back arriving Irish. The exodus went on and on. In 1603 a Pembrokeshire landowner reported that the coastal parishes had been flooded with arrivals from Ireland fleeing from 'the late wars'.

This was a reference to the recently concluded campaign which had resulted in O'Neill's defeat in 1601 at Kinsale. The earl's plight was replicated in thousands of other human tragedies. The destitute, unemployed soldiers who had followed him and their families set sail for England and the continent searching for shelter and food.

Unsurprisingly, we know far less about this class of emigrant than we do about their aristocratic countrymen. As we have noted, the Flight of the Earls was not the last gasp of the Old Irish, the pre-Reformation Irish aristocracy. In 1641 another great rebellion broke out. It started as an attempt by the dispossessed Gaelic Irish of Ulster to regain their lands but turned into an alliance of all the Catholics of Ireland to defend their religion and preserve their rights against new assaults on their standing. Catholics still had property to defend. At this point, despite plantations and confiscations, they held two thirds of the cultivable land in the island. They felt, however, that they could be dispossessed at any time. By continuing to refuse to accept the spiritual as well as the temporal authority of the monarch they were deemed untrustworthy and potential traitors. The rise of Puritanism in England in the first half of the seventeenth century led to further attacks on their faith. After the start of the Ulster rebellion in 1641, in which 2,000 Protestant settlers were killed and tens of thousands driven out, the Puritan Parliament decreed the absolute suppression of Catholicism in Ireland. The eleven years of the rebellion ended with its ruthless extinction by Cromwell. It is calculated that by the end one third of the population had been killed. Many were transported as slaves to the West Indies. Those who survived were, as Robert Kee puts it, 'sentenced in their own country to a life of social ignominy and handicap'.

Under Cromwell another great land grab took place. Most of the best acres were taken away and given to Protestant adventurers and settlers, some of them distributed to Cromwell's soldiers in lieu of back pay. By the end, the economic standing of the Catholics had been devastated. It was the Protestant minority now who held three-quarters of the cultivable land, with the Catholics being shunted across the Shannon to Connaught, the poorest of Ireland's four provinces.

The restoration of the monarchy in 1660 and the accession of Charles II raised some hopes among the Catholic Irish that their lands might be restored to them, but it was not to be. The Protestant Ascendancy, as the landed class of nobles, gentry and peasantry came to be known, had nothing to fear. No substantial change was made in the Cromwellian settlement. Scholars estimate that by the time of the restoration Catholic landownership was down to one fifth, most of it in the less prized soil of Connaught. With the arrival of Charles's Catholic brother James on the throne in 1685 as King of England and Ireland, the Catholics might reasonably have hoped that their fortunes were set to improve. A Catholic, Richard Talbot, Earl of Tyrconnell, was appointed to govern Ireland as lord lieutenant. He set about raising a large and almost entirely Catholic army

Siege at Drogheda, 1641. Later the town was sacked by Cromwell and the civilian population massacred. (Painting by Marcus Stone, 1840–1921)

The siege of Derry, 1690.

which James summoned to join him. The alarm this occasioned among the Protestant establishment was one of the factors that led to James's overthrow in the Glorious Revolution of 1688, which placed William of Orange on the British throne.

The following year, on 12 March James arrived in Ireland from France, intent on winning back his kingdom. His forces under Tyrconnell held the whole island with the exception of Derry and Enniskillen. The scene was set for yet another war between the forces of the Catholic natives and the Protestant settlers. This one was to be decisive. The stakes were set high by the Catholic parliament appointed by James II in Dublin which attempted to reverse the trend of the preceding century by passing an act repealing the Cromwellian settlement and confiscating virtually all the property of Protestants in the kingdom, albeit with compensation. The act never had time to come into force, but it had a traumatizing effect on the Protestant Ascendancy, who were to look back on it as proof of what they might expect were Catholics ever to gain the upper hand.

Paranoia entered the Protestant mind-set and endured. Two hundred years later a British official could write that the attempt to reverse the Cromwellian settlement 'gave the Protestant proprietors a fright from which they have not properly recovered even to this day ... they seem to think that they only garrison their estates, and therefore look upon the occupiers – I cannot call them tenants – as persons ready to eject them on a favourable opportunity'.

So it was all or nothing. Despite the advantage of numbers the Irish army supporting James was ill equipped and badly trained. The French supplied advisers but, preoccupied with their own wars, could spare little in the way of troops. It was anyway already clear to them who was going to win. The French war minister wrote: 'Whatever good intentions the Irish may have for the preservation of their country and their religion, if they fight with three-foot sticks against the troops of the Prince of Orange which will have swords and muskets, they will soon be killed or forced to fly.'

And so it turned out. Derry, which was besieged by the Jacobite forces, was relieved by an English fleet. William of Orange himself arrived in Carrickfergus on 14 June 1690 and a little over a fortnight later defeated James's forces at the Boyne. James fled

Governor's house

Cannon
defences

Tavern

Customs
house

THE GOVERNOR'S HOUSE

The governor is keen to follow European fashion and style. He likes to live very elegantly in this large, imposing house. He often hosts sumptuous parties and balls for the wealthy citizens of the town.

Bedchamber

Pirate captain presents treasure to the governor.

Prison cell

Armourers

Inside the customs house

to France, leaving his supporters to their fate. The Irish, with some support from the French, fought on for another fifteen months. The Jacobite army was defeated again at Aughrim in July 1691. In October the stronghold of Limerick fell to the Williamite forces and the resistance was over.

The failure of the campaign can truly be said to have sounded the death knell of the old order in Ireland and the beginning of a long period of disadvantage and persecution for the stubborn majority who would stick to the old religion. Kee writes that the disasters of the Boyne and Aughrim 'marked the beginning of a long period, fading slowly in intensity over the centuries ... in which to be Catholic in Ireland meant automatically to be the underdog. To be Protestant meant, whatever one's status and by no individual effort of one's own, to be automatically superior.'

The O'Briens judge the fate of the Irish to have been inescapable.

The tragedy could not have been averted, or even notably softened, by the wisdom or humanity of any ruler. The people of Ireland had been caught and crushed in the play of international and ideological forces: the English Reformation and its insecurity, the Counter Reformation and its quasi-millenarian hopes ... English and Irish, pressed into closer contact by these forces, discovered how diversely history had formed them. Each side reacted to this discovery with that ethnocentric reflex of shock, disgust and anger, which is among the strongest and most terrible forces in human history. The weaker party was doomed to be oppressed, and the weaker party was the native population of the smaller and more remote island.

The cause lost. The flight of James II after his defeat at the Boyne. (Painting by A.C. Gow)

The Battle of the Boyne, 1690. The Twelfth of July victory is sacred in Ulster Protestant memory. (Painting by Jan Wyck)

Seventeenth-century engraving of the Protestant champion: William of Orange and his queen, Mary, in 1690.

The surrender of Limerick had been agreed under terms which gave Catholics a wide measure of toleration, guaranteeing the rights they had enjoyed under Charles II. Under pressure from the now Protestant parliament in Dublin, supported by English opinion, William gave way and set in train a series of penal laws that were continued by his successors, Anne and the first two Georges, depriving Catholics of the right to sit in parliament or vote for it, and excluding them from the law, the universities and all significant offices and forbidding them to possess arms or a horse worth more than five pounds. The higher clergy were banished and no Catholic could keep a school.

The penal laws were devised in support of a political and economic as much as a religious end. They served to reinforce the Cromwellian land settlement which had put the territorial wealth of the country overwhelmingly in the hands of Protestants loyal to the crown. The Catholic population was needed as cheap labour, but it was necessary to build a legal stockade to keep them in their place and prevent them from regaining possession of their old land.

The man who commanded the garrison when Limerick fell, Patrick Sarsfield, did not wait to see William betray his promises. Under the Treaty of Limerick, he and those who had fought with him were free to leave the country. More than 10,000 did so. These men were the founders of the Wild Geese — the legendary band of exiled Catholic chevaliers who were to roam Europe in the succeeding decades, fighting in the armies of Catholic kings, keeping alive the notion of old Irish chivalry and valour and with it the hope of liberation from the English. If the earls of Tyrone (O'Neill) and Tyrconnell had made up the first flight, the second was more significant. Their leader, Sarsfield, became a substantial figure in song and poem. In some ways he acts as a repository of certain conceptions of Irishness, not all of them flattering. There was no doubting his courage and daring. However, the Duke of Berwick gave a cool appraisal of his overall military worth. 'He was no general but a mere cavalry officer,' he wrote, adding more generously, 'a handsome fellow if you like, a fine, good natured, generous, irascible Irish giant, exceeding even his own dragoons.'

The remarks of Berwick, who later married Sarsfield's widow, were amiably intended no doubt, but the tone is unmistakably *de haut en bas.* We know what Berwick means to say — that Sarsfield was a decent enough fellow, but a loser. Tyrconnell, the Jacobite commander, had a similarly reserved opinion. A French general, trying to press Sarsfield's case for promotion, recorded that Tyrconnell had resisted, 'saying he was a very brave man but he had no head'.

The Sarsfields were a classic mixture of Norman and Gaelic stock. An ancestor had been a standard-bearer to Henry II, and others had fought alongside subsequent

English kings. Patrick was probably born around 1650 and studied as a young man at a French military college, probably taking part in Louis XIV's campaign against the Dutch in 1672 and not fetching up in Ireland again until the 1680s, when there are various accounts of him getting into scrapes and duels before finding his place in history in the doomed Jacobite War. He distinguished himself with a number of daring escapades including the destruction of a supply train that thwarted an early attempt by William on Limerick.

Sarsfield was one of the signatories to the Treaty of Limerick. His deeds have been recorded by one of his men, Gerald O'Connor, who followed him into exile. They marched to Cork and boarded ships bound for France. 'Our transports dropped slowly down the stream of the Lee,' he wrote, 'its shores stretching in desolate plains for miles.' The Irish troops disembarked at Brest, where they waited in vain for French support to mount an invasion of Ireland. Later Sarsfield and his troops, in alliance with William's enemies, were able to do battle with the King's forces in the Low Countries. In 1693 Sarsfield died a soldier's death in the service of Luxembourg fighting the Dutch at Landen. The faithful O'Connor was there to record his last moments. 'The noble form of the hero lay on a pallet in a hut. He feebly lifted up his nerveless hand and gave me a letter.... It read: "I am dying the most glorious of deaths; we have seen the backs of the tyrants of our race. May you, Gerald, live to behold other such days; but let Ireland be always uppermost in your thoughts."'

It is easy to see in Sarsfield the embodiment of a tradition that was embraced by all classes of Irish manhood. He was reckless, a warrior, preferring the action of battle to the strategic calculation of generalship. His approach would characterize much of the subsequent military efforts to rid Ireland of the English. An anonymous poem written not long after the Jacobite War summed up the melancholy of the defeat and departure:

> Many a soldier, all proud and gay,
> Seven weeks ago they passed this way
> With guns and swords and pikes on show
> And now in Aughrim they're lying low
>
> Kelly's Aughrim has manure that's neither lime nor sand
> But sturdy young soldiers stretched over the land
> The lads were left behind on the battlefield that day
> Torn like horsemeat by the dogs where they lay
>
> Overseas they all are, Ireland's best
> The Dukes and the Burkes, Prince Charlie and the rest
> And Captain Talbot their ranks adorning
> And Patrick Sarsfield, Ireland's darling.

Patrick Sarsfield. (Seventeenth-century painting, Irish School)

·4·
THE WILD GEESE

IN THE END some 30,000 soldiers left Ireland following the signing of the Treaty of Limerick in October 1691. Their departure denuded Ireland of the people best equipped to protect native rights. The loss that was felt is apparent in the very name by which the exiles were known. Legend had it that the souls of the dead soldiers returned to the old country in the form of migrating geese. The Wild Geese, the romantic nickname given to the post-Limerick exiles and other military refugees forced by political and religious circumstances to make their livings by their swords in foreign armies, were to endure many disappointments, indignities and betrayals in the long years that they and their descendants soldiered on foreign fields. Few of them were ever to set foot in Ireland, even though they were to nurture a continuing loyalty to the place for a remarkable length of time. Indeed the Irish displayed a continuous capacity for steadfastness even in the support of manifestly unworthy leaders. James II had already displayed his cowardice by his flight to France after the Boyne. Now he showed his treachery to the men who had followed him, bilking them of their proper pay.

Once in exile the Irish were divided up into four regiments and were soon engaged on the French side in Louis XIV's endless wars with his neighbours in the later part of the seventeenth century as he sought to extend France's frontiers. Occasionally they were able to come up against their real enemy, fighting with the French against William's forces at the siege of Namur and with the Duke of Luxembourg at Steenkirk and at the battle of Landen, where Sarsfield was killed in 1693. These engagements were supposed to be the precursor of an invasion attempt. Louis gave his support to a plan

(*Left*) The battle of La Hogue, 1692. (Late nineteenth-century painting by George Chambers) (*Above*) Irish troops were scattered throughout Europe after the War of the Spanish Succession.

5 2

IIII

Maresh^l Tallard &other French Gen^{ls} br^o Pris^{rs} on to England

French generals captured during the War of the Spanish Succession pictured on a set of commemorative playing cards.

to invade Ireland, defeat William and restore James to his throne, a move that if it succeeded would fatally undermine the forces of the League of Augsburg, the defensive alliance created by William with Spain, Sweden and German princes against France.

An invasion plan was agreed upon and a force assembled early in April 1692 in Normandy between Cherbourg and La Hogue commanded by James and the Duke of Berwick, his illegitimate son. The venture was founded on optimism and James's unsupported belief that the admiral of the British fleet, Russell, would abandon William and come over to him. Russell did no such thing and destroyed the French fleet off La Hogue on 24 May. The 13,000 Irish troops in the expeditionary force were soon scattered throughout Europe, spreading themselves among the French armies in Flanders, Germany, Spain and Italy. Even at this stage the logic that sustained the optimism of the Wild Geese was being subjected to the strain of experience. In Spain they were fighting for France against a Catholic dynasty that the Irish had in the past looked towards to deliver them from the English. Not only that, they were to find themselves pitched against Irishmen, the descendants of soldiers who had fled with O'Neill and entered the service of the Spanish monarchy. At the battle of Ter, the records show a Viscount Clare with the French. An Earl Clare was known to be serving on the Spanish side, leading to speculation that father may have been fighting son. During the subsequent War of the Spanish Succession, Irishmen faced Irishmen at the battle of Cremona in 1702. The engagement provided a story that illustrates the great confusion of loyalties that the Wild Geese faced. The French were ranged against a wide alliance including the Austrians, the Dutch and the English, who were all opposed to the idea of the Spanish throne passing to a grandson of Louis XIV and the consequent agglomeration of French power. At Cremona the French forces, which were supplemented by units of the Irish Brigade, the official Irish element in the French army, were attacked by the Austrians. Among the Austrian emperor's ranks was an Irishman called Francis MacDonnell. He appears to have entered the Austrian army through his uncle's connections with the Austrian court. There was already a well-established Irish link with the Austrian military. Colonel James Butler commanded a regiment in the imperial service in 1630 and, after an influx of Irish mercenaries from the Polish army in 1638, Irish officers made up the biggest foreign contingent in the emperor's army.

MacDonnell distinguished himself by capturing the French commander, de Villeroy, who offered him 2,000 crowns a year and his own regiment if he released him and came over to the French side. According to one account, recorded by the historian of the Wild Geese, Maurice Hennessy, MacDonnell was outraged at the proposal and replied that 'he had hitherto served with fidelity; he would never be disgraced by perfidy; he preferred honour to fortune, and hoped to attain by honourable services in the Imperial army the rank offered to him by the French as the reward of treachery'.

A little later MacDonnell figures again in the account, this time in a rather less creditable role. His commander, Prince Eugene of Savoy, sent him under a flag of truce to address the soldiers of the Irish Brigade in the French ranks. MacDonnell passed on the prince's offer of higher pay if they changed sides. He urged them to accept the terms. Otherwise, he said, 'I do not see how you can escape certain destruction. We are in possession of the whole town except your part. His Highness waits my return only to attack you with his whole force and cut you to pieces if you do not accept his offers.' MacDonnell's approach was politely but firmly rejected.

MacDonnell went on to do well in the imperial service, as did many other soldiers of fortune as we shall see. But, although the history of the Wild Geese is replete with success stories, life was tough and insecure at the lower end of the military scale. The soldiery learned early on not to put their faith in foreign princes. In the brief interlude of peace provided by the Treaty of Ryswick in 1697, which ended the French war against the League of Augsburg, the Irish found that their services were no longer required by Louis XIV. The Irish Brigade was already firmly in the army, so it was the other Irish units scattered through the military that bore the brunt of the royal cost-cutting. The non-commissioned officers were hit hardest. Penniless and largely ignorant of the language, many of them had no recourse but crime, becoming footpads and robbers. One contemporary wrote that 'the route between St Germains [where the Jacobite court was situated] and Paris was not safe because of them and they added murder to robbery when they met with resistance'. If caught they could expect no mercy; the punishment was being broken alive on the wheel.

The officer class might have had some means but their plight was still unenviable. By the Treaty of Ryswick Louis acknowledged William as the legitimate monarch of England. The consequence was that the exiles could forget ever regaining their lost lands. Nor could they return home easily, being technically under pain of death (though we shall find that some individuals in fact did so). The disappointment must have been devastating. One can only wonder at the temperate tone of their appeal to Louis' generosity, in which they pointed out that they had 'served in France with a zeal scarcely differing from that of the King's natural subjects'. Their restrained eloquence had some result and the officers were formed into a special corps for use at the royal discretion.

By the end of the War of the Spanish Succession few illusions were left to the Wild Geese. Maurice Hennessy notes that 'it became increasingly obvious to them that they were the merest ciphers in the European cockpit. Their bitterness must have been even more painful as they observed the two nations in which they had placed their hope for a free Ireland [France and Spain] at each other's throats.'

Periodically there were events that raised their spirits, such as the expeditions of the Old and Young Pretenders in 1715 and 1745. But the Stuarts were an unreliable enterprise in which to invest hope. The fidelity to the cause of Ireland and Catholicism remained remarkably constant, however. The ideological underpinnings of what were at face value mercenary activities were demonstrated at the 1745 battle of Fontenoy, a major encounter in the 1740–8 War of the Austrian Succession, in which the French took on the English. The French forces contained six regiments of the Irish Brigade, those of Clare, Dillon, Bulkeley, Roth, Berwick and Lally. There was also a separate cavalry regiment under Fitzjames.

The English (among them Irishmen in the service of King George II), under the Duke of Cumberland, appeared to be winning, braving murderous French fire to advance up the slope to the village of Fontenoy. The Irish troops were thrown forward to halt the advance by smashing through Cumberland's right flank, composed of guardsmen. Before battle was joined there was a curious harking back to ancient times when a guards officer and, from the Irish side, one Anthony MacDonough from County Clare met in single combat. The Englishman had his sword arm smashed and was thereby forced out of the battle. Then shouting, 'Remember Limerick and Saxon Perfidy' the Irish ran yelling into battle. According to the French account, the Irish charged with fixed bayonets and the fighting was hand to hand. The English faltered and then fled. Most historians agree that it was the Irish action which carried the day. The losses on the Irish side were very heavy. Thirteen officers including the Chevalier Dillon, commander of the Régiment de Dillon, were killed and 261 men, out of a force of 3,870, and 383 were wounded.

The victory acquired a significance far greater than its importance as a feat of arms. For a defeated nation, beaten down by the discriminatory laws that followed William's failure to ratify the Treaty of Limerick, backed by the perpetual threat of violence, it was a welcome sign that the underdog could bite back. The flood of literary celebration continued down almost to the present day and Fontenoy was seized on by the republican movement as proof that the British could be defeated by physical force. The battle gave rise to quantities of stirring and mawkish verse, most famously that of Thomas Davis. It is hard to dispute his poetic speculation that it was the pure blue flame of revenge that drove Irish feet forward that day, righteous rage at the wrongs that had been visited on them and their own.

The finest hour of the Wild Geese: Fontenoy, 1745. (Painting by Felix Philippoteaux, 1815–1884)

How fierce the look these exiles wear, who're wont to be so gay
The treasur'd wrongs of fifty years are in their hearts today
The treaty broken, ere the ink wherewith 'twas writ could dry
Their plunder'd homes, their ruin'd shrines, their women's parting cry
Their priesthood hunted down like wolves, their country overthrown
Each looks as if revenge for ALL were stak'd on *him* alone
On Fontenoy, on Fontenoy, nor ever yet elsewhere
Rush'd on to fight a nobler band than these proud exiles were!

Another epic, *With the Wild Geese*, by Emily Lawless, fantasizes in macabre fashion about seeing a ghost ship peopled with the white corpses of the dead arriving on Erin's shore, home at last – a variation on the homing spirit at the heart of the mythology of the Wild Geese.

Austrian dragoons. Irish adventurers did well in the service of the emperor.

Soldiering in the service of foreign kings was undoubtedly a risky business, but the rewards could be high. Fitzjames, the Irish cavalry commander at Fontenoy, was ennobled and became a marshal of France. Later he entered the Austrian service and became a count, field marshal, imperial chamberlain and councillor of state. The armies of France, Spain and Austria offered an opportunity for advancement, while enabling them to remain faithful to principle and religion, to young Irishmen who had no chance to achieve their potential in their homeland. The penal laws ensured there was a steady flow of recruits. Nicholas Taafe, member of a family that prospered spectacularly in the Austrian empire, described his motives for the move in a petition to the emperor Franz Stephen and Maria Theresa. He had left, he said,

because he was afraid that his descendants pressed by the penal laws would not resist the temptation of becoming Protestants. He therefore took refuge to a Catholic country where his ancestors were well known by the military service they had rendered at different intervals to the House of Austria. He had abandoned his relations and his estate and the rank and liberty he had in his own country to prevent his descendants from deserting a religion to which their Imperial majesties so fervently adhered.

The historian John McGurk has pointed out the remarkable penetration the Irish achieved of the continental military and political elite:

General Ricardo Wall was minister of foreign affairs in Spain under two monarchs successively from 1754 to 1763; in Austria at roughly the same time Field Marshal Count Francis Maurice Lacy was president of the council of war; in France, Charles O'Brien, Earl of Thomond, was made *maréchal de France* in 1757. On St Patrick's Day 1766 in Vienna, Count O'Mahony, the Spanish ambassador at the Austrian court, gave a party at which the guests included Count Lacy, Generals O'Donnell, Maguire, O'Kelly, Browne, Plunkett and McElligot; four chiefs of the Grand Cross, two provincial governors, several knights military and four privy councillors all claiming Irish descent.

The court and the army were not the only options. James Smith McGavan from County Longford was knighted by the empress Maria Theresa for his services to the study of medicine at the University of Prague, while French military records from early in the eighteenth century show discharged Irish soldiers going into education as teachers of law, philosophy, rhetoric, mathematics and the classics.

The Irish regiments were to soldier on for more than 120 years in all. In Spain the last three, the Hibernia, the Irlanda and the Ultonia, were disbanded in 1818. Before that, the French Revolution had sealed the fate of the remaining regiments of Dillon, Berwick and Walsh. Later the future Louis XVIII was to pay an elegant tribute to the last of the Wild Geese. Presenting a standard he offered it as a 'pledge of our remembrance, and a monument of our admiration, and of our respect; and in future, generous Irishmen, this shall be the motto of your spotless flag: "1692–1792, Semper et Ubique Fideles"'.

Membership of the upper classes amounted to a sort of continental freemasonry, so for the officers absorption into society in a foreign country was not as daunting as might be expected. Of the social fate of the lower classes not a great deal is known. Relatively few women travelled with the first shipments of Wild Geese after the surrender of Limerick, so we can presume that some of the soldiers must have made local liaisons. Intermarriage and interbreeding are the quickest routes to racial assimilation, and many of the offspring of the exiles must have been absorbed into the host nations within a generation or two. Some of the Wild Geese actually made it home. There is a happy ending to the story of Anthony MacDonough, who beat the Englishman in single combat before Fontenoy. Sent back to his native Clare to recruit more Irishmen for the Irish Brigade (a dangerous commission risking imprisonment and death), he met a young woman, fell in love with her and never went back to France.

The pain of exile for the Wild Geese could to some extent be balanced by the excitements and adventure of the military life of the times. Hennessy recounts the stories of two who left behind tales that could easily form the basis of novels, one of them picaresque, with their extraordinary mixture of drama, colour and the vagaries of fortune. Gerald O'Connor was a member of an ancient Offaly family who fought with Sarsfield and was one of the thousands who left for France after Limerick, received a commission in a French cavalry regiment and spent several years soldiering on the Rhine. His entry to France had been eased by his friendship with a French Huguenot called de Bacquancourt, who was attached to the Williamite forces and whom O'Connor had captured and held prisoner. The relationship was evidently very cordial, for when O'Connor was forced to release his prisoner after the fall of Limerick, de Bacquancourt told him that he would ensure that his Catholic brother would take care of him when he arrived in France. A letter duly reached him inviting him down to the family château in Normandy. During his stay there he encountered his host's daughter Estelle, fell in love with her and, despite the opposition of the girl's mother, married her in his twenty-ninth year. The marriage was a long and happy one, blessed with five children and interrupted only by O'Connor's frequent trips to the field.

He fought against the British at Ramillies in 1706, taking part in an unsuccessful attempt to capture Marlborough, and two years later was at Oudenarde, another British victory. He ended up an army inspector, retiring at the age of sixty in 1731. He comes across as a decent, conservative, somewhat humourless man, easily shocked by displays of irreverence. He witnessed the funeral of Louis XIV and reported that 'the funeral procession was ill-attended and mean; the people along the roads showed at best indifference, ribald jests and murmurs were occasionally heard. Such was the end of a reign of unparalleled grandeur; it proved how utter is the vanity of earthly things but it was discreditable to the character of the French nation.' After he left the army his eldest son John, who had joined one of Lord Clare's regiments based in Rouen, gave a dinner for him to mark his retirement. The old soldier noted with dismay that not one of those present remembered Sarsfield or knew very much about him.

But his biggest disappointment had been his return to Ireland. Somehow O'Connor was able to return openly. He did so in 1725, landing near Dublin, and quickly formed a poor impression of the city which he had not seen for thirty-five years. After the splendour of Paris he found the capital dirty, squalid and small, a collection of narrow alleys and lanes which he thought reflected the subjugated status of his race. He stayed six months and seems to have had an unsettling time. The political situation depressed him. He wrote that the penal laws 'placed the Irish Catholic in a position of permanent and degrading bondage, in some respects worse than when he was under the iron rule of Cromwell'. His own people had largely decided to conform and collaborate with the colonizing power. The only good time he seems to have enjoyed was with the companions of his deceased old friend and wife's uncle, de Bacquancourt, who had ended his days in a Huguenot community in Portarlington.

Drunkenness and dirt. Dublin as it appeared to the fastidious and successful Wild Geese émigré, Gerald O'Connor. (*Dublin* by John Nixon, 1760–1818)

Despite his disappointment he was to return fifteen years later to visit his brother. His two sisters had already died in a convent in Kerry, and the country was recovering from a famine caused by the failure of the potato crop. He then went back to France and died there eight years later. In his memoir he laments that he would 'never see the dear land again, nor yet the few remaining kinsmen of our race'. He sings the praises of France, to which he owes 'all that makes life most prized — a wife, who has been the best of helpmeets, sons, daughters, friends, companions, home; I love her as if she were a second mother'. Yet he says his thoughts go back to 'our fallen Offaly, to the scenes of my boyhood and first youth, to the castle by the lake, to our broken clansmen, to the parents of two generations who nursed me on their knees'.

O'Connor's story is very revealing, for though he belonged to the upper classes and his background is far from typical among the great mass of Irish emigrants, the essential features of it are echoed in the stories of many. For one thing, he treats exile as an opportunity, surmounts his difficulties and finds love, employment and honour in the host country, which he adopts as a second home and to which he gives unstinted loyalty. But simultaneously he retains a great love of the land of his birth. Eventually, though, this love becomes a sort of quasi-mystical attachment. The Ireland he dreams of is transformed by time and distance into a mythical realm. When he is confronted with the reality he is stunned with melancholy and disappointment. He presumably had the opportunity to resettle at home. But he prepares to live out his days in France, with rose-tinted memories of his childhood in the castle by the lake.

O'Connor was clearly a decent man. Legend would have it that all the Wild Geese were like him, brave, honourable and upright. The evidence that this was not always so is provided by another altogether racier memoir, recorded by a contemporary, Peter Drake. Drake's story is remarkable for its frankness as the rogue narrator recounts his unscrupulous and amoral meanderings through the period. In a way he provides a useful counterpoint to the instructive life of O'Connor. An émigré can take two basic routes when confronted with the dangers and hardships of exile, one straight, one crooked. Drake had no hesitation in taking the latter.

The prison at Cork where Wild Geese soldier Peter Drake spent some time, not all of it unpleasant.

Like O'Connor he left Ireland after Limerick, but on arrival in Brest he was deemed by the French to be too young for military service and was dispatched by his patron Lord Trimlestone to the home of the Marchioness of Catulan to learn the language. He was later forced to leave her household, apparently after some discreditable incident, and sought help from the mother of Patrick Sarsfield, who was living with her two daughters in straitened circumstances in the Jacobite colony at St-Germain-en-Laye. Next he tried his luck with his kinsman the Earl of Limerick, but there was another falling out and he joined up with Colonel Arthur Dillon's regiment of foot. At one point, in 1699 he took the foolhardy step of returning to Ireland. On arrival in Cork he was recognized as one of Sarsfield's men and thrown into prison, where he spent six months awaiting execution. Prison life was not too onerous. He was allowed visitors, in particular a young woman called Elizabeth Toomy. 'I had the pleasure of seeing my benefactress at least twice a week, and sometimes oftener,' he recalled. With her help he escaped and made his way to

Dublin, where he lived high on the hog, apparently not pressed by financial concerns. Eventually he returned to France, served with the French against Marlborough at Ramillies and was wounded at Malplaquet in 1709, another great British victory.

Drake was a restless spirit. In 1707 he pops up in Dunkirk, part of a crew of French privateers attacking English shipping in the Channel. He was captured and sentenced to death for treason, but the sentence was later commuted to life imprisonment. Once again the prison regime was lax and he was allowed out of the Marshalsea to go drinking and whoring. His success with women extended across the social scale. Amazingly, through the intercession of male and female friends at court, he was granted a royal pardon by Queen Anne in 1709. He returned to the military life, this time as a sergeant in Marlborough's army, and was posted to Ghent. Somehow he managed to amass a fortune, which he dissipated on wild living on his return to London. It was his practice there to put up only at lodgings where there was no man about the house in the hope that he would be able to share the mistress's bed. Encountering a rich, middle-aged Dutch widow he decided to seduce her. He tricked her into a sham marriage and used her money to set up a successful inn which he later handed over to a confederate called Mrs Jolly, who turned it into a brothel. Drake's villainy is somewhat mitigated by the cheerful frankness with which he recounts his misdeeds. Recalling the seduction of the Dutch widow he describes their first meeting when he took a room at her lodging house. 'The widow came in. She was a little plump woman about five-or-six and fifty, was well-dressed and had the remains of a good face.... I fixed my resolution and waited for the first favourable opportunity to make a general attack, which soon happened. The storm was made in the dead of night and after some faint resistance I entered.'

Drake gives us a glimpse of an encounter with anti-Irish prejudice in London, though how widespread such feeling was is not revealed. Sipping his pint in a London alehouse he encounters a certain Captain Hardyman whose reputation as a virulent hater of the Irish has come to Drake's ears. 'He was not ten minutes in the room before he began to suck his breath through his nostrils, as if taking snuff, swearing, damn him, he smelt an Irishman. I heard one of those who sat at the next table say, "Now the game begins." In a very little time the Captain repeated his words again. I looked very earnestly at all the company and was sure there was no Irishman in the room but myself ... I called for a fresh pint of ale, got up and walked very gravely towards him.' Announcing his nationality he said he intended to wash away the offensive smell – and flung his pint in Hardyman's face. The captain failed to respond in

It was in a London alehouse in the early eighteenth century that Peter Drake met with anti-Irish prejudice. (*The Press Gang* by John Collett, 1725–80)

kind. Surprisingly the two later served in the same British regiment and became friends. Or perhaps it is not so surprising. Drake's career showed that he was not one to adopt rigid postures in the daily struggle with life. He had the true resilience of the successful émigré, and like some successful exiles he regarded the law lightly. In the end he returned to Ireland, where his charm seems to have sustained him, gaining him entry to the homes of the gentry where he appears to have lived out his last days as a perpetual, peripatetic house guest, dying at the age of nearly eighty.

Occasionally in the records of the military exiles we catch sight of the women who went with them, their wives and lovers. A considerable number seem to have accompanied or followed their menfolk, after the Flight of the Earls, to Spain. Researches by Micheline Walsh in the Spanish archives have revealed a succession of petitions to the king concerning their rights as widows or military wives and lists of the pensions paid, generously it would seem, from the royal coffers. The women show themselves to be tenacious, persuasive and confident of their rights, and there are echoes of Queen Medb of legend in the forthright but silky tone of their appeals. One written in 1607 by Rosa Guegan (Geoghean), living in north west Spain, declares that she is the recipient of a pension of twelve crowns a month. 'But now my brothers and my sons have gone to serve Your Majesty in Flanders so I am sad and lonely. So I humbly beg Your Majesty to order that my pension be paid to me in Flanders so that I may go and receive it there as punctually and fully as I have received it in Galicia.'

Bolder still is Catherine Magennis, Countess of Tyrone, fourth and last wife of Hugh O'Neill, who on his death in 1616 in Rome managed to persuade the king of Spain to pay her the same grant he had made to her husband. The O'Neill family in Ireland were angry and tried to divert the money. Apparently they had some success, for Catherine was forced to write a letter complaining that she has not been paid for seventeen months. Bemoaning her condition she fears 'less to die of hunger than to become the ridicule of the English enemies for they say that my husband the Earl of Tyrone waged war on them at the instigation of King Philip II and his son, Your Majesty, leaving his king and losing his estates in Your Majesty's service and that now Your Majesty is without concern for this afflicted and unprotected widow who was his wife and leaves his family to die of hunger.' The letter is signed 'Your Majesty's most humble servant', but the tone of the letter is far from humble. Rather it is the voice of a proud, indignant woman using what amounts to moral blackmail to get her rights.

The women of the Wild Geese seem a spirited bunch. The nature of warfare at the time gave them little opportunity to express that spirit in action. One scrap of history, though, provides some evidence of what they might have been capable of. It concerns Lucy Fitzgerald, resident in the Catalonian town of Girona, which was garrisoned by 400 troops of the Spanish regiment of Ulster. When in 1808 a 6,000 strong French force arrived to besiege the town she organized a women's unit called the Company of Santa Barbara and put herself at the head of it. Its duties were to transport ammunition and food to the troops and care for the wounded. The first attack was seen off but the town fell a year later. A witness describes how Lucy and her companions worked calmly under a storm of shells, carrying the wounded and laying them down on the bloodsoaked floors of the hospital. Lucy herself reported that 'all ranks behaved with distinction. They administered untiringly to the needs of the defenders at the various points of attack. They brought much needed water and brandy to the fort of Monjuich and carried back the wounded on litters and in their arms. Despising the dangers of shells and bombs which rained about them without stop, they displayed heroic zeal, charity and supreme courage.'

The exploits of the Wild Geese have received wide attention in Irish studies, partly because of the colourfulness of their story, partly because of the wealth of material relating to them. Their story contains many characteristics of the émigré experience that we will see reproduced in the histories of other, more mundane exiles. The military adventurers may have left their homeland but they possessed a durable, physical force; patriotism that fate determined was never put to decisive practical use. Nonetheless they peformed a number of useful functions in keeping native Irish hopes alive and in providing a friendly environment for future generations of Irish rebels seeking to enlist foreign powers, particularly France, once again in their cause. The claim that Ireland was always in their thoughts has perhaps been exaggerated by Irish propagandists with little in the way of military achievement to boast about. But the words of Arthur Griffith, writing when Irishmen were engaged on the Boer side in the war with the British, nonetheless have the ring of truth.

> Oh Mother of the Wounded Breast
> Oh Mother of the Tears
> The sons you loved and trusted best
> Have grasped their battle spears
> From Shannon, Lagan, Liffey, Lee
> On Afric's soil today
> We strike for Ireland, brave old Ireland, Ireland far away

Officers of the Irish Brigade who fought the British in the Boer War.

· 5 ·

THE FIRST IRISH AMERICANS

SOME TIME IN 1586 an Englishman, Captain Ralph Lane, travelling near what is now Edenton, North Carolina, recorded in his diary that 'an Irishman, serving me, one Edward Nugent, volunteered to kill Pemisapan, King of the Indians. We met him returning out of the woods with Pemisapan's head in his hands and the Indians ceased their raids against the British camp.' This laconic entry appears to be the first written reference to the presence of an Irishman in what is now the United States. In the following century some 50,000 to 100,000 men and women left Ireland for the North American colonies and 250,000–400,000 in the years 1700 to 1776. The numbers were smaller than the great exoduses of the following century but they represent a significant proportion of the Irish population, which stood at less than two and a half million in the middle of the eighteenth century.

Most, maybe three quarters, of the emigrants in the first period were Catholics, with the rest made up of Anglicans and a sprinkling of Quakers and Ulster Presbyterians. In the next century, though, the pattern shifts. Catholics were then only a fifth to a quarter of the emigrant host. A further fifth were Anglican and the rest Dissenters, with Ulster

Presbyterians predominating. Thus, as the great historian of Irish emigration Professor Kerby Miller has pointed out in his monumental work, *Emigrants and Exiles*, 'early Irish emigration to North America was highly unrepresentative of the religious composition of Ireland's population'.

It was the Catholics who were most likely to be impelled by economic circumstance to leave their homeland. The condition of the Catholic poor, the overwhelming majority of the native population,

(*Left*) The Old Country. Conviviality survived poverty. (*A Shebeen at Donnybrook* by Erskine Nicol, 1825–1904) (*Above*) Across the ocean a very different culture was waiting. (*Pilgrims Going to Church* by George Henry Boughton, 1833–1905)

The New World as mapped by the Cabot brothers in 1497.

remained dismally constant throughout the period from the end of the Jacobite War to Gladstone's land reforms of 1870 and 1881 – a period of nearly 200 years. Foreign visitors to Ireland reported with depressing consistency the appallingly low living standards of the bulk of the peasantry. The Protestant Dean Swift in 1720 judged the condition of the Irish tenant to be worse than that of an English beggar. Another Protestant, the philosopher Bishop Berkeley, wondered 'whether there be upon earth any Christian or civilised people so beggarly, wretched and destitute as the common Irish'. Even the chief government official in Ireland wrote to the king in 1770 expressing his concern about the state of the mass of people. 'What with the rapaciousness of their unfeeling landlords and the restrictions on their trade, they are among the most wretched people on earth.'

The ghastliness of existence for the majority of the population is only too well attested to. Cottiers – those who received a cabin and a scrap of land in return for labour service – small tenants and landless labourers made up three quarters of the rural population. A parliamentary committee in 1835 calculated that three million people were exposed every year to the possibility of absolute destitution. They were stunted by malnutrition and ravaged by epidemics of typhus and dysentery. Their diet was of potatoes, occasionally softened with the addition of a little buttermilk. In the immediate pre-Famine era up to 1845, when the potato crop could supply only 75 per cent of the food needs of the labouring, the extremely poor faced starvation between late spring and the harvest, eating sometimes only every other day, preferring their potatoes half raw so as to slow down the process of digestion. They lived in one room shacks with mud floors without chimneys or windows. Families slept together, bundled up in straw on the floor. They dressed in rags and went barefoot.

Occasionally conditions would improve as the slow commercialization of the Irish economy brought benefits, a few of which trickled down the steeply banked social scale. But the amelioration was largely illusory. The demographic growth that the commercialization stimulated – Ireland's population was to rise from 2.3 million in the mid eighteenth century to 6.8 million by the time of the 1821 census – did not reflect any structural improvement in the economic security of the masses.

The essential injustice of the Cromwellian land settlement persisted. As well as imposing harsh restrictions on Catholic rights, the Dublin parliament in 1695 abolished customary Irish tenure, which made farmers who did not have formal leases tenants on sufferance, essentially squatters on land they might have worked for generations. Protestant landlords abolished the old communal *clachan* farmlands, threw out the tenants and fenced in the land for pasture. The opportunities that were provided in the late eighteenth and early nineteenth centuries by the expansion of the Irish economy, in response to a growing need in Britain for food and clothing for its growing urban population and to sustain its military operations overseas, were not available to the great majority of the Irish people. For many, nothing they could have done would have improved their situation. Landlords and visitors complained frequently of the fecklessness and laziness of the Catholic poor, managing to blame their condition on the victims' own shortcomings. But cultivation of the potato patches took only three months of the year and paid labouring work on other people's land was in short supply. Apathy and despair were endemic. It was little wonder that people sought solace in the *poitín* bottle or left the land and took to the roads as vagrants and beggars.

Urban flight was not an alternative. Ireland's backwardness ensured that towns stayed small – in 1841 only 20 per cent of Ireland's eight million population lived in communities containing more than twenty houses – and life was even less appealing than in the countryside. Beyond the stately walls of Protestant Dublin's public buildings and elegant residential squares the city was vile, stinking and disease ridden, with half of its children dying in infancy.

Interior of the Old Lutheran Church in York County from a sketchbook, *c.* 1800.

Even those who had managed to haul themselves above the mass by acquisition of an education or a trade had not necessarily discovered an escape route for the penal laws blocked the translation of learning into a paying occupation, and craftsmen suffered from local restrictions such as those in force in Armagh in 1770 which barred Catholics from the occupations of trader, shopkeeper and craftsman.

In the circumstances, as Professor Miller observes, 'the inexorable processes of commercialization and population growth ultimately gave the majority of Irish only two logical alternatives: permanent emigration abroad or rural pauperization at home'. As he goes on to point out, 'it is singular that so few Catholic Irish emigrated to colonial America'. It was a phenomenon that surprised contemporaries. In 1669 an immigration official trying to lure Munster peasants to Carolina remarked that they were 'loath to leave the smoke of their owne cabbin if they can but beg neer it'. A century later, the agriculturist and traveller Arthur Young stated that 'Catholics never went; they seem not only tied to the country but almost to the parish where they were born.'

The reluctance of the Catholics to seek the opportunity of emigration at this stage is not easily explained. The possibilities were there as the North American colonizers' labour needs created a substantial demand for indentured servants, and agents were constantly seeking human resources to plant in the new lands, apparently regardless of religion. Agents haunted country fairs offering passage to the 'Land of Promise' where 'freedom, peace and plenty' were waiting for the migrant and his or her descendants and the message was further disseminated in handbills and newspaper notices.

An unusually sympathetic depiction of the emigrants' plight from *The Lady's Newspaper*, 1849.

Yet (leaving aside the preponderance of Catholics among the seventeenth-century colonial settlers) by and large they seemed intensely reluctant to go, even when economic hardship was particularly pressing. In 1740–41 crop failure produced a famine in which starvation and disease killed 200,000–400,000 people, yet there seems to have been no exodus comparable to the flood of emigration that followed the Great Famine of 1845–50.

The obvious political explanation for this reluctance was that the new territories were English and Protestant and the culture was Anglophone at a time when the peasantry were still mostly speaking Irish. Why exchange one English plantation for another, far away? But antipathy to the notion of departure lay deep. Christianity and Anglicization had failed to remove place, hearth and soil from their central place in Gaelic culture and the Gaelic psyche and land in some ways continued to define identity. Bards and Catholic clerics disparaged the idea that there was any virtue in seeking one's fortune abroad if it meant abandoning the homeland. In addition, historians have discerned in Gaelic culture a bias against the spirit of individual enterprise and innovation that drives the successful émigré. The ranks of disapproving foreigners travelling in Ireland who fastidiously recorded the condition of the Irish peasantry in the period made much of their lack of initiative. 'If you expect from them individual volition,' an English journalist warned, 'or enterprise of any kind you will fail.' They are frequently presented as children, charming, noisy, affectionate, but lacking any sense of direction and responsibility, and ultimately exasperating and in need of being taken firmly in hand.

Certainly in Gaelic culture there was a passivity and a resistance to materialism that could not have been more out of tune with the great themes of the rising capitalist age. Fatalism and acceptance were a way of dealing with a wretched life. The cultural inheritance of the Gaels encouraged such a world view. Visitors frequently recorded examples of the stoicism of the poor. One was told that 'we must be patient with what the Almighty puts upon us'. Another peasant declared, 'we are under the mercy of the world and a poor mercy it is, hard living and little pay and the workhouse and the grave at the end of it all'.

Folk tales deprecated material achievement and taught the lesson that the acquisition of wealth often had adverse consequences. At the end, said a traditional song,

Poverty was borne with resignation and good humour in Irish culture.

even for the richest man, 'little goes with him to the grave but a little sheet of a shroud and a narrow wooden coffin'. So the struggle beyond what was needed for subsistence was futile. And the lack of material comforts was compensated for by the pleasure of one's family and neighbours and the ancient pastimes of tale-telling, cracking jokes and drinking. It is hard to gauge happiness at the best of times but, leaving aside the melancholy that pervades much of Gaelic culture, the Catholic poor seem to have borne their misery with remarkable good nature. There are several travellers' tales that bear witness to an innate sense of hospitality that belongs to another, ancient era. Caught in the wilds, the Chevalier de la Tocnaye stayed one night in a cabin where:

> half a dozen children, almost naked, were sleeping on a little straw, with a pig, a dog, a cat, two chickens and a duck. I never before saw such a sight. The poor woman told me her husband was a sailor, that he had gone to sea three years ago, and that she had never heard from him since. She spread a mat on a chest, the only piece of furniture in the house, and invited me to lie there … It rained very hard and I knew not where to go so I lay down on this bed of thorns. The animals saluted the first rays of the sun by their cries and began to look about for something to eat. The novelty of my situation amused me for a moment. I transported myself in imagination into the ark and fancied myself Noah. It would seem that I appeared as odd to these animals as they did to me, the dog came to smell me at the same time showing his teeth and barking. The pig also put up her snout to me and began to grunt, the chickens and duck began to eat my powder bag and the children began to laugh. I got up very soon for fear of being devoured myself. I should add that I had no small difficulty in making my hostess accept a shilling.

There were many similarities between the oppression of the poor in Ireland and African slaves in the West Indies; and for Irish emigrants to the West Indies, their lot was unlikely to improve under the harsh conditions imposed by the plantation owners.

An American traveller, Asenath Nicholson, was given similar hospitality by a poor couple whose daughter had been his servant in New York. She wrote that he had 'slept under rich canopies in stately mansions of the rich, in the plain wholesome dwelling of the thrifty farmer ... and under tents on the hunting ground of the Indian, but never where poverty, novelty and kindness were so happily blended'.

Despite the strong tug of home, hunger and hopelessness drove many to leave. The first wave of transatlantic voyagers of the seventeenth century went largely as indentured servants. Their destinations were not only the American colonies but the West Indies, which were being settled by the English and to some extent the Irish. The terms of the contract were that the worker promised to fulfil several years of bonded labour in return for his passage and some material reward when the service period was over. By the 1620s, ships were sailing regularly from Cork and Kinsale carrying food and textiles and servants to trade for West Indian sugar and Chesapeake tobacco. The Catholics' presence was recorded in all the mainland colonies but particularly Virginia and Maryland, where tracts of land were set aside for them called New Ireland and New Munster.

Settlement in the West Indies was encouraged by Irish born governors, and by 1666 a fifth of the whites in Barbados were Irish Catholics. A little later, in the Leeward Islands, they made up a third of the free population and in Jamaica in 1731 the governor calculated that Irishmen and women made up the bulk of the lower classes. Emigration to the islands seems to have brought little in the way of prosperity and good fortune to the emigrants. The terms must have appeared attractive to a landless man. In exchange for seven years' labour on the plantation, servants would receive their passage, food, clothing and shelter and at the end receive a sum of money – 'freedom dues' – and a parcel of land. But relations between the usually

Protestant planter elite and the Catholics were often bad. The growing numbers of immigrants alarmed the owners, who feared political subversion and tried to impose tight controls on the servants. There were frequent crop failures and the tobacco and cotton were often inferior to what was being grown in the American colonies.

Many labourers found their conditions hard to bear and there were outbreaks of drunkenness, insubordination and escape attempts. The planters responded to indiscipline with brutality, stringing men up by their hands and lighting matches between their fingers in one recorded torture. In Barbados, the declining revenues from cotton and tobacco persuaded planters to turn to sugar in the 1650s. The success of the switch led to expansion and the swallowing up of arable land. Land values trebled. Landlords began to renege on their obligations to provide labourers with land at the end of their stint. The tensions between the two classes were increased by the arrival of prisoners transported from Ireland by Cromwell in the 1640s after his bloody campaign against the rebels. The Irish could discern little difference between their situation and that of the black slaves. One servant, Cornelius Bryan, was sentenced to twenty-one lashes on his back by the public hangman in Bridgetown for uttering a mildly seditious remark. In 1673 a grand jury reported that 'the severity of some of the masters and overseers towards Christian servants has been such that some have been largely destroyed'. A 1667 report described the Irish in Barbados as 'poor men that are just permitted to live ... derided by the negroes and branded [with] the epithet of white slaves'. They worked 'in the parching sun without shirt, shoe or stocking ... domineered over and used like dogs'. Even when free of their obligations they found that the scarcity of land and competition from slave labour forced them into a struggle for existence that can hardly have been preferable to the circumstances they left behind. Some managed to haul themselves into the ranks of the landed. In the late seventeenth century, 10 per cent of Jamaica's property owners were of Irish extraction. That may sound more impressive than the facts merited, however, for only a handful seem to have reached the status of 'middling planter'.

The concentration of land into fewer hands and the growing reliance of the plantation owners on African slaves forced the immigrants to consider their futures. Many servants and labourers and smaller landlords decided to try their luck elsewhere and left the West Indies for North America, and particularly the early settlements of South Carolina. The conditions on the mainland were frequently as harsh as those on the islands. Indeed the whole experience of emigration at this time for the poor was one that they were lucky to survive. In the seventeenth century perhaps a third of white settlers died on the Atlantic voyage or in the first years of acclimatization. The governor of Virginia testified that in the early years of the colony four-fifths of indentured labourers died in the first year from disease, from the effects of the climate or from overwork. In addition the Catholics had to endure religious and racial abuse. The hostility of the Protestants of New England to the Catholic Irish was so great that few considered settling there. Religious antagonism was codified in legislation to prevent Catholics practising their religion. Professor Miller states that 'Catholicism was at best barely tolerated before the American Revolution.'

News of the conditions somehow filtered back, reinforcing the existing cultural resistance to the blandishments of the labour agents. In 1669 one complained of the

In the eighteenth century, Lynch's justice entered the language.

The town of Lynchburg.

difficulty of luring Catholic servants from Munster to South Carolina. 'I could not obteyne any,' he wrote, 'for the thing at present seems new and forraigne to them … they have been so terrified with the ill practice of them to the [Caribbean] Ileands where they were sould as slaves, that as yet they will hardly give credence to any other usage.' Miller has observed that those who did go seemed to be 'rootless, restless men, already estranged from the communal, familial and cultural ties which kept the bulk of their countrymen at home'. If they did get married they were absorbed into Protestant, colonial networks. Pervasive anti-Catholic attitudes meant that very few retained the stigmatizing 'O' or 'Mac' prefixes to their name. These circumstances ensured that the colonial Catholic Irish never coalesced into ethnic communities which maintained the transatlantic links needed to facilitate large-scale emigration.

There were some success stories. As everywhere at the time, the chances of success were greatly increased by the support of a patron, and not all masters were cruel. Charles Lynch ran away from school in Ireland as a teenager and ended up an indentured servant in Virginia in the early 1700s, working for a planter called Christopher Clark. He seems to have been treated by Clark as a son and he ended up marrying his daughter. Clark also granted him a stretch of land along the James River to farm. At the time of his death Lynch was a respected man in the colony and he gave his name to the town of Lynchburg, which sits on what was his land. His son Charles was brought up as a Quaker, the religion of his mother. The pacifist sect became alarmed at his belligerence towards British authority and expelled him from the society in 1776. This Lynch was a friend of Thomas Jefferson and a member of the House of Delegates. He played a key part in mobilizing Virginia's resources in the preparations for the War of Independence fought between 1775 and 1783. He became a colonel in the militia and fought the British at the battle of Guilford Court House in North Carolina in 1781.

Lynch's name is remembered for another reason, however. As a justice of the peace in the extra-legal courts that operated in the absence of the British courts, he was notorious for the swiftness with which he conducted proceedings and the near certainty of conviction — after which the defendants were usually whipped. Many of those who appeared before him were accused of being accomplices of the British. If acquitted they were set free with apologies. If found guilty they were strung up by their thumbs from a walnut tree outside his house in what is now Altavista, Virginia, and flogged until they shouted 'Liberty for ever'. His reputation for rough justice meant his name became associated with the practice of summary mob executions, though in fact Lynch seems to have preferred the lash to the rope. His house, named Avoca after the mystical Irish vale immortalized in Thomas Moore's ballad 'The Meeting of the Waters', has been preserved as a historic landmark. Moore himself was the son of a Dublin grocer who was born in 1779 and registered as a Protestant to allow him an establishment education at Trinity College. Although a friend of the United Irishman Robert Emmet (a member of the United Irishmen movement which sought to make Ireland a republic independent of Britain) he played no part in revolutionary activities, but spent most of his life in England, where he studied law and attempted to enter society. Nonetheless his sweet, melancholy verses with their themes of exile and the past struck a deep chord with Irish émigrés, particularly in America. Songs and poems like 'The Harp that Once through Tara's Halls', 'Flow on Thou Shining River' and 'Come Rest in This Bosom', though they made little mention of the harsh realities of the life the exiles had escaped, were sung by them to evoke memories of the old country and pass on an idea of it to younger generations. Irish Americans erected a memorial bust to the poet in Central Park in New York in 1880.

General John Sullivan.

The American Revolution provided Irishmen with a means of bearing arms against their historic enemy and many seem to have been eager to take it. The rosters of American regiments contain a large number of Irish names, some of whose holders distinguished themselves in action. The first major military engagement of the war, when rebels seized British powder and shot from a magazine at Fort William and Mary in New Hampshire in 1774, was led by John Sullivan, a descendant of one of the Wild Geese who had fetched up in America. The following year Captain Jeremiah O'Brien, son of an émigré from Dublin, commanded the *Unity*, which captured the British gunboat *Margaretta* off the coast of Maine. Colonel William Thompson, the founder of the Battalion of Pennsylvania Riflemen, regarded as the linear ancestor of the present United States army, was a native of County Meath.

One of Thompson's soldiers, Timothy Murphy, was born in New Jersey in 1751, shortly after his parents arrived there from Donegal. Later they moved west to Pennsylvania, which was still frontier country, and Murphy grew up as a backwoodsman earning a reputation as an excellent shot. After serving at the siege of Boston and the battle of Trenton in 1776, he was posted to a regiment of sharpshooters. His hour of fame came at a turning point in the revolution at the battle of Saratoga in the autumn of 1777, when rebels were facing the army of the British commander, Burgoyne. British resistance was being stiffened by the actions of a Scottish general, Simon Fraser. Murphy's commander pointed him out to him with the words, 'That gallant officer is General Fraser. I admire him, but it is necessary that he should die. Do your duty.'

Nineteenth-century engraving of the heat of battle at Saratoga, 1777.

Murphy obliged, missing with his first two shots but mortally wounding the General in the stomach with the third, before going on to dispose of his aide de camp. Seeing Fraser fall, Burgoyne quit the field, and ten days later surrendered his entire army, giving the rebels a significant victory. The Ancient Order of Hibernians put up a monument to Murphy at the spot where the shots were supposed to have been fired, in 1913.

The war also provided opportunities for Wild Geese regiments in the service of the French and the Spanish, who were allied to the emergent United States. The regiments of Dillon and Walsh from the Irish Brigade of the French army were at Yorktown, the last major battle of the Revolution, which took place in 1781. The Regimiento de Hibernia from the Spanish army played a vital role in the defeat of the British at the battle of Pensacola during the Gulf Coast campaign of 1780–1. Not all Irishmen were on the side of the rebels. Some fought in the ranks of the crown, and it is worth remembering that the first St Patrick's Day Parade in New York was organized by the Sons of Ireland, a loyalist regiment in the service of the British, on 17 March 1779.

The presence of the Irish generally at the centre of the struggle against the British is reflected in the fact that three of the signatories to the Declaration of Independence in 1776, Matthew Thornton of New Hampshire, and George Taylor and James Smith of Pennsylvania, were Irish born. Other signatories were of Irish descent, including the sole Catholic, Charles Carroll of Carrollton, Maryland. The Carrolls are an interesting example of aristocratic emigrants who made rapid progress in the nascent political structures of emerging America as well as building a fortune. They claimed descent from princes and in spite of their religion had somehow managed to retain their position and wealth until 1688, the year of James II's overthrow, when the first of them came to Maryland.

Charles Carroll was born in his father's house in Annapolis, a substantial property which contained a chapel, the first Catholic place of worship in the town. He and his cousin John were educated at the Jesuit school in Baltimore, then at St Omer in France (John was ordained). Debarred by his religion from public life, he took little part in politics until the Revolution. He was the author of a series of anonymous newspaper articles attacking the tax levied to support the Anglican Church and become well enough known in revolutionary circles to be asked by the Continental Congress of rebel colonies to join a delegation which set off to Quebec in a failed attempt to try to persuade the Canadian colony to join forces with the thirteen American colonies. After election to the Continental Congress he signed the Declaration of Independence and helped draw up the Maryland state constitution and its bill of rights. He opposed the confiscation of British property, saying that it would be to reproduce the tyranny of the state which the nation was rebelling against. At the turn of the century he retired from public life and dedicated himself to his estates. He lived long, straddling the transition of America from colonial infancy to adolescent world industrial power, turning the first spadeful of earth in the construction of the Baltimore and Ohio Railroad in 1828. On his death he was probably the richest man in the United States.

His cousin John was a vigorous campaigner to remove the disabilities imposed on Catholics by British rule. When the war ended he drew up a 'plan of reorganization' for the American Catholic Church and in 1785 was appointed prefect-apostolic by Pope Pius VI and, five years later, became the first Catholic bishop of the United States. Among his achievements was the foundation of a seminary so that American candidates for the priesthood would not have to travel to Europe to study, and the building of Baltimore's cathedral. Carroll's energies were much needed. Separated

An Irish dynasty. Charles Carroll of Carrollton.

Signing the Declaration of Independence, 1776. (Painting by John Trumbull, 1756–1843)

from the conventions of home, many Irish Catholic males in the colonies drifted away from the Church. Spread through a largely Protestant population, freed from the pressures of conformity that they were subjected to at home, they either adopted host religions or became, as Carroll was to complain, 'name only Catholics'. In 1783 there were only 25,000 practising Catholics of all nationalities in the whole country, even though up to 100,000 had arrived from Ireland alone since the beginning of the century.

The success of the Carrolls and the pride Catholic Irish Americans took in their achievements is an indication of the Catholics' minority status among the ranks of Irish immigrants in America at the time of the revolutionary upheavals. The majority were Protestants, among them many Presbyterians from Ulster. They began to arrive in the American colonies in the second half of the second decade of the eighteenth century and between 1717 and the Revolution some 200,000–300,000 had settled in Pennsylvania, Virginia and, especially, the Carolinas. Irish Protestant emigration began to overtake that of Catholics in the last decades of the seventeenth century and from the start of the eighteenth century to the start of the revolutionary war three-quarters of the emigrants were Dissenters and Anglicans. Of these, 70 per cent were Ulster Presbyterians. Anglicans were the smallest group. Given their dominant status in Ireland, their wealth and near monopoly in politics and the professions, there was little to lure them overseas. Among those who did go were younger sons seeking their fortunes. But the great majority were the lower orders, tradesmen, small tenant farmers and labourers, fleeing from the hostility and resentment of the Catholic majority and towards the promise of a new land. A few, like George Taylor, the Declaration of Independence signatory, who started out as an indentured labourer at a Pennsylvania iron furnace, were markedly and visibly successful. It is difficult to distinguish the Anglicans' social progress as they were soon swallowed up by the surrounding English community.

The Ulster Presbyterians, though, strove and for a while had considerable success in preserving their cultural identities. They kept in touch with the old country and established lines of emigration that allowed the foundation of distinct communities, congregating in settlements with names like Colerain, Donegal and Fermanagh. The glue for this social cohesion was provided by the tightly structured organization of the Presbyterian faith. Religion, or rather religious oppression, was often advanced as the reason for the Presbyterians' flight. It is true that Dissenters suffered from penal legislation in Ireland, notably the Sacramental Test Act of 1704 which barred Presbyterians from civil and military offices and closed their schools, churches and burial grounds. Many of the people who left in the great exodus of 1717–20 were led by their ministers, whose presence did much to hold the communities together in the New World. In fact there seems to be little causal link between the legislation and the decision to leave, and the policy was anyway subsequently softened by various indemnities until the act was finally repealed in 1780.

The Presbyterians' bible-based world view with its tribal treks and uprootings to escape injustice and intolerance might have provided a contextual framework for the migrations, but the fundamental impulse for the exodus was largely economic. The first substantial emigrations, which began in 1717, were at least partly the result of the expiry of land leases offered to Scottish Presbyterians by landlords in the early years of the previous century to lure them to the plantations of Ulster. They had been given on generous terms. When they terminated, many proprietors amalgamated holdings and doubled and tripled rents. In addition there was a succession of bad harvests (in the eighteenth century about a third of all harvests were bad) and outbreaks of disease. Many decided to cut their slender ties with the province and move on. There was another exodus between 1725 and 1729, caused by further crop failures and rent rises. Farmers growing for the linen industry were granted shorter leases by landlords who wanted to tie their income more closely to their economic circumstances and each renewal usually meant an increase. In considering the misery of Ireland at the time it is well to remember that existence could be wretched for non-Catholics too. One witness spoke of the roads of Ulster crowded with the destitute 'scarce able to walk and infinite numbers starved in every ditch'. Some went to Britain but others signed on as indentured servants. The growing linen industry provided a

means of crossing the Atlantic. Most Ulstermen travelled to ports along the Delaware river such as Philadelphia, Chester and New Castle in the holds of ships that were returning home having off-loaded their cargoes of flax seed.

From 1730 to 1769 about 70,000 Ulster Presbyterians sailed the Atlantic, most of them poor smallholders, artisans, cottier-weavers and labourers. Emigration cost money. In the middle of the period, a passage cost from £3 5s to £9, including provisions. In addition it was necessary to have a minimum of £10 for inland transportation, fees for land grants, seeds and tools and the wherewithal to survive until the first harvest. The expense meant that half the emigrants were individual males or indentured labourers. Nonetheless, unlike the Catholic emigrants of the time, whole families did travel together as did single women looking for husbands, further reinforcing blood links on settlement.

For most the risks and costs of emigration were worth it. It was the inability to wrest a living from the land, together with a perceived religious and political persecution, which had driven them out. In America there was land aplenty, with no question of leases, rents, tithes and taxes. Taming it was backbreaking and dangerous work, with the threat of disease, wild beasts and snakes and the native inhabitants. But most colonists succeeded in making a life for themselves that was significantly richer materially than what they had left behind. One Robert Parke boasted that Pennsylvania 'abounds in fruit. Scarce an house but has an apple, peach and cherry orchard'. Even the labourers sustained themselves on 'a pint of rum beside meat and drink of the best for no workman works without their victuals in the bargain'. There

Their greene corne.

Corne newly sprong.

Their sitting at meate.

The place of solemne prayer.

The house wherin the Tombe of their Herounds standeth.

SECOTON.

A Ceremony in their prayers w
strange testurs and songs dansing
abowt posts carued on the topps
lyke mens faces.

was a certain amount of condescension and even hostility to contend with from longer-established Protestant settlers. But the message that the Ulster Presbyterians sent home was that America was a fine country, a place of opportunity not exile where, like some Old Testament tribe, they could live a Christian life untroubled by ungodly authority or grasping landlords.

The self-conscious collectivism of the Presbyterians' approach to settlement meant that their distinctiveness lasted a little longer than that of other immigrant groups. Assimilation was more rapid in towns than in isolated areas. Old customs persisted – such as the firing of guns at weddings, an intimidatory gesture from the old country, aimed at their Catholic neighbours, to whom weapons were forbidden. Weddings and wakes were bibulous affairs. At the end of the eighteenth century some still spoke Lallans, the dialect of the Scottish lowlands. Despite the presence of Presbyterian ministers, the kirk's grip on the community rapidly weakened. By 1800 only 15,000 American adults were members of Presbyterian churches. Ministers seem to have been scarce in the frontier areas where many of the Ulster Irish settled. In their absence, the immigrants became Methodists and Baptists.

There were similarities in the impulses which drove both Catholic and Dissenting Irishmen and women to cross the Atlantic. Both were fleeing economic and religious oppression. But there were distinct differences in the way they approached the experience. There has been much conjecture that the Presbyterian mind-set, its emphasis on the value of material gain and its reverence of hard work and individual effort, better equipped the Ulster emigrants for the rugged life of the frontier. In fact, the Ulster Scotch-Irish, as they liked to call themselves to distinguish themselves from the other emigrants, shared much of the Gaelic collectivist spirit of the Catholic community in Ireland. Nonetheless, their experiences in the new land seem to have been happier than those of the Catholics who made the journey. Professor Miller explains:

> whereas Catholic emigration was largely a trickle of footloose individuals, culturally or circumstantially divorced from traditional bonds, Protestant emigration – especially Dissenter emigration – was a mass movement, a social exodus. Had Catholic experiences in colonial America been more positive, more departures would perhaps have occurred; certainly the creation of a cohesive and self-satisfied Ulster-America offered inducements to subsequent emigrants which the scattered, submerged and largely down-trodden Irish Catholics in the New World could not provide … Before 1776 experiences abroad only served to reinforce a traditional native Irish world view which stigmatized emigration to America as less desirable than poverty and persecution in Ireland.

That perception was about to change.

(*Opposite*) **A sixteenth-century Indian village: the native people the colonists were displacing. (Sixteenth-century illustration by John White)**

·6·

ACROSS THE ATLANTIC

I N MAY 1844 Martin Murphy and his family, together with a group of other settlers, gathered at Council Bluffs, Iowa, to attempt a 2,000-mile journey across harsh, unsettled territory to what they hoped would be the Promised Land of California. The expedition reflected an extraordinary spirit of courage and optimism. Two previous attempts to drive wagon trains to California had ended in failure in the deserts of Nevada. Along the way there were only a few colonial outposts, forts maintained by fur companies, where they could expect help. Their high hopes were eventually realized. The Murphys ended up super-rich ranchers, billionaires in contemporary terms, owning great swathes of territory and thousands of head of cattle – but not before they had endured one of the most harrowing journeys of pioneering history.

Martin Murphy was born in Wexford in 1785, farming as a tenant on what appears to have been a reasonable-sized holding, marrying Mary Foley in 1805 and having six children with her before emigration. The likelihood is that the decision to leave Ireland was in reaction to the economic pressures resulting from the enormous demographic growth that had increased Ireland's population by 75 per cent between 1780 and 1821. Martin

and Mary and four of their children set sail for Quebec in 1820. The fare to British North America was much cheaper than a ticket to the United States and most Irish emigrants made landfall in Canada before moving south. The Murphys however stayed, buying land in Frampton, south-east of Quebec, having three more children and being joined by those they had left behind. The children grew up and had children of their own. They lived near each other, operating as a clan, replicating the communal life they had shared in Ireland.

(*Left*) Nineteenth-century settlers fording a river in Oregon.
(*Above*) Clearing the land in North Carolina.

Starting out. A settler family in Nebraska, 1870.

In 1840 the extended family decided to move *en masse* in search of better soil and a more clement climate. This time they settled in Missouri, buying land in Holt County. They were followed by some of their friends and relatives from Canada and the settlement became known as Irish Grove. But only four years later they were on their way again. The land was better than the soil they had left behind, but malaria was rife in the area and in 1843 carried off Martin's wife Mary and his son Martin Jr's daughter. A priest comforting the family in its bereavement spoke enthusiastically of California where there was good land for the taking. Furthermore, it was ruled by Mexico, and Catholicism was the established religion. Martin Sr decided it was time to move on yet again.

The Murphys had with them on the expedition Elisha Stevens, an experienced backwoodsman, and an old trapper and his two half-Indian sons acted as guides. The fifty-strong party set off in eleven ox-wagons and crawled through Indian country at two miles an hour, making fifteen miles a day. By November they were nowhere near their destination and the snows were coming. Intelligently, they decided the best course was to stay put and wait for spring, and the main party butchered the cattle, built a cabin and hunkered down for the winter while the fittest went ahead, returning to rescue them in March, by which time they had been reduced to eating hides. All the members of the expedition survived. Martin Murphy died aged seventy-seven in 1884, the owner of 92,000 acres of prime California land and much real estate in the cities of San José and California, patriarch of one of the richest families in the state.

The coolness of the Murphy party was in contrast to the conduct of the later expedition of the Donner party who in the winter of 1846–7 were also caught in the snows in the High Sierras. Of the eighty-seven-strong party, thirty-nine died. Of the Murphy party, half were Catholics. In the Donner party there was only one Catholic family, that of Patrick and Margaret Breen from County Carlow and their seven children, all of whom survived. The Breens too seem to have behaved intelligently and farsightedly, fighting despair with prayer. They went on to become substantial citizens in California. The stories of the Murphys and the Breens have been cited as an example of how the Catholics' collectivist way of dealing with crises could prove to be the best survival strategy. As we have noted before, though, a collective approach was not unique to the Catholics of the Irish diaspora and was a feature of Presbyterian societies in America.

The argument over whether Gaelic Catholic values and behaviour patterns were a handicap in the raw, individualistic world of the emergent United States is one that will never be resolved. In some cases, as we will see later in the progress of the Catholic Irish in the big cities, the collectivist approach could bring advantages. The history of the likes of the Murphys proves that, given sufficient energy and resourcefulness and a certain amount of luck, the agreeable image of America as a land of milk and honey could eventually become reality.

During the period up to Ireland's Great Famine of the 1840s perceptions of emigration began to change among the Catholic Irish, and they started to edge a little closer to the view of Protestant and particularly Presbyterian travellers that emigration was an opportunity rather than a painful necessity and cause for lamentation. Letters home painted a rosier picture of the prospects that attended anyone bold enough to make the voyage. Padraig Cundun of upstate New York, owner of a 'fine farm of land', bragged that no landlord 'can demand rent from me and my family and I can eat our fill of bread and meat, butter and milk any day we like throughout the year'. For Catholics and Dissenters there was the further attraction of the absence of an established church, with its attendant demands for tithes to support it. Tithes represented a major financial burden on a peasantry already staggering under the weight of rents. Patrick Breen's widowed

News of life abroad. (*The Letter from America* by James Behan, 1837–1904)

Departure from the Old Country.
(*The Emigrant Ship* by Edwin Hayes, 1819–1904)

mother was forced to pay £4 14s 11d a year in tithes to the Protestant Church of Ireland, the equivalent of a labourer's pay for six months. Artisans and skilled workers, if they were lucky, could set themselves up within a very short time of arriving. A weaver boasted that he had bought a house and land worth $200 within the space of three years, having arrived with half a dollar in his pocket. Even labourers were told by advertisements seeking road and canal builders that they could earn a wage that would keep them in the comfort enjoyed by a substantial farmer at home.

Between 1827 and 1832 Ulster non-Catholics still made up about half the number of emigrants to North America, following what were by now well established routes into the security of established communities. But, as the 1830s wore on, relatively poor Catholics from Munster, Leinster and Connaught overtook them. They were smallholders, younger sons denied land by the increasing practice of retaining farms intact rather than dividing them up, and labourers who had done well enough to scrape the fare together or who had received a remittance from a previous emigrant. By 1831 the fare disparity between British North America and the United States had narrowed and the standard fare from Ireland to Canada was only £1 10s and to America £2 to £3. It is clear that even these prices were a deterrent and that many more would have gone to America if they could. Instead they sought relief in another direction, heading east to England or Scotland. Between 1830 and 1835 about 200,000 paid a few pence for deck passage across the Irish Sea and by 1841 about 400,000 had settled in London, Manchester, Glasgow and other cities.

Those sailing to Liverpool for onward passage to America were the target of swindlers and conmen who preyed on victims, many of whom had never ventured further than their ancestral townland before taking the decision to emigrate. Often ships did not set sail for weeks after the advertised time and the emigrants' funds dwindled away as they waited for departure. For many, hopes for a new life in America ended in a Liverpool slum. British Passenger Acts were meant to impose minimum standards on shipowners operating transatlantic passages to prevent overcrowding, but these were often ignored, and until the middle of the eighteenth century many of the ships carrying emgrants were old, slow and unseaworthy. Boats sank or had to turn back to port because they were shipping water. The voyage took about six weeks and was for most people an ordeal. The poorest passengers were allotted only two square feet of space in steerage and the height of the decks made standing upright impossible for adults. People slept four to a berth and in stormy weather, when the hatches were battened down, huddled together in suffocating misery. Sanitary

Voyagers entertained themselves between decks during the long transatlantic passages.

conditions were vile. Protestant passengers expressed their disgust at their sometimes lice-ridden and unhygienic Catholic fellow travellers, 'the most ignorant and degraded mass of human beings with whom I had ever been brought into contact', in the view of one Ulster Presbyterian. The stench below decks could be abominable. Sexual shenanigans and drunkenness were rife. In these cramped, overcrowded conditions there were considerable risks from typhus, cholera, dysentery and smallpox. When they struck, mortality rates could go as high as 25 per cent. Few vessels carried a doctor and there were few facilities for treatment on board. The food and water on offer were often bad and, as the emigrants' own stores ran out, unscrupulous captains charged extortionate prices. There were inadequate cooking facilities and the constant threat of fire from the stoves.

There was nothing to do. Occasionally an iceberg, a whale, a shoal of flying fishes or the sight of a distant sail would send passengers rushing to the rails. Most of the time they were bored. They played cards, danced – and drank. There were fre-

The Irish gained an early reputation for rowdiness in comparison with more docile newcomers, as depicted in this satirical cartoon, 'Uncle Sam's Lodging House'.

quent quarrels and fights between Catholics, Orangeman and English Protestants. Storms were frequent, and no voyage seems to have been completed without one, bringing the passengers – whatever their faith – to their knees to beseech the Lord for deliverance. There was the risk of being driven by the winds into the fog and rocks of Newfoundland. The sight of floating driftwood or a flock of birds was greeted with joy and relief and passengers spent hours on deck straining for the first sign of land. 'The exciting cry of "Land! Land!" ran through the ship like wild fire,' one emigrant recalled. 'Such were my feelings vacillating between hope and fear that I could hardly believe it.'

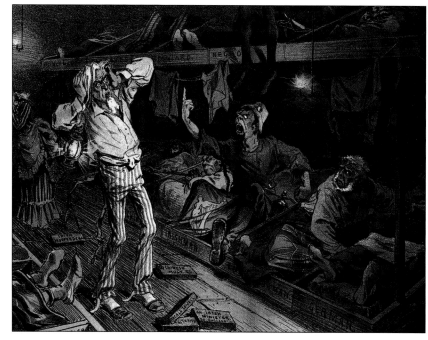

Digging the Erie Canal in Lockport, New York. On arrival in US cities, the work was hard and dirty.

Once on dry land, the emigrants' troubles were not necessarily over. When Mary MacLean arrived in Quebec in 1832 she found herself in the middle of a cholera epidemic, with people dropping dead in the streets and the hospitals overflowing. Everything depended on one's contacts. Chain migrants, those going to join family members in an existing community, could expect a joyous welcome and the warmth of familiar faces and a familiar culture in an alien land. For the individual, from the depths of the Irish countryside, without family or friends to comfort and sustain him, the culture shock must have been traumatic. Of the unskilled arrivals, some were young women going to work as domestic servants in the homes of the rising American bourgeoisie. Many of the young men became labourers, working in city-building and great communications enterprises like the Erie Canal, which was opened in 1825 between Albany and Buffalo, New York. It might well have been called the Eire Canal, for it was dug largely by Irish labour. The canal was the brainchild of Governor DeWitt Clinton. Hiring agents waited at the docks to recruit young Irishmen as they disembarked. A historian of the canal, Lionel Wyld, writes, 'the Irish proved to be the greatest of boons in digging the Ditch ... Few people could stand the conditions which the Irish labourers tolerated. Local inhabitants, Pennsylvania Dutch and Negroes from the South, were all tried but the Irish bogtrotters always proved the best of the lot.'

Their appearance spread alarm among the white natives. A housewife in Oneida County exclaimed that 'Mohawks and Senecas we have survived, but these strange folk look fitter for crime than for honest work. I misdoubt that we shall find ourselves murdered in our beds one fine morning.' This prophecy proved to be innaccurate. The Irish fought among themselves, often over work, but there is little record of crimes against the locals. Most of the young men had never worked in construction before, being farming lads. They took to it quickly and became contractors and subcontractors on the canal. They bid for the contracts to dig stretches of the waterway, building shanties as they went which replicated the villages they had left behind, down to the cabins and a patch for potatoes.

In the cities, life for the unskilled was often little better than what they had left behind. 'The Irish labourer very rarely attains independence,' noted a European observer, 'changing only the nature of his toil from the hackney coachman to the porter … or the hired drudge.' They huddled together in small, insanitary slums nicknamed Paddytowns, drinking together, fighting outsiders and hustling for work. Sometimes the exploiters were their own kind, like the entrepreneur, saloon-owner and slum landlord Hugh Clark of Philadelphia, who paid his weavers pitifully low wages for their piecework. The jobs the labourers did were not merely exhausting. They were dangerous, sometimes fatally so. A middle-class Irish immigrant sympathetically wondered: 'How often do we see such paragraphs in the paper as an Irishman drowned — an Irishman crushed by a beam — an Irishman suffocated in a pit — an Irishman blown to atoms by a steam engine — ten, twenty, Irishmen buried alive in the sinking of a bank — and other like casualties and perils to which honest Pat is constantly exposed in the hard toils for his daily bread.'

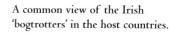
A common view of the Irish 'bogtrotters' in the host countries.

The poor Catholic Irish found themselves in a society that, no matter how much it might require their muscles, often treated them with contempt. There was an innate, structural hostility to Catholicism among established Americans. 'This is an English colony,' wrote Charles O'Conor, son of an émigré United Irishman. 'People inherit from their ancestors the true Saxon contempt for the Irish.' The libertarian ideology and rhetoric of the Revolution had failed to translate into social tolerance, and the America of President Andrew Jackson, son of Ulster immigrants, was increasingly divided and factionalized. Jackson, a Tennessean lawyer, was the dominant political personality in the United States between the Revolution and the Civil War,

strengthening the power of the executive over the legislature and the federal government over the states. He placed little emphasis on his Presbyterianism. Within the immigrant world, though, the strong presence of Presbyterians and Protestants meant that the sectarian bigotry of Ireland was transplanted and flourished in the soil of America. 'Papists' or 'Papishes' were routinely abused as dirty, violent, superstitious and ungodly, *Undermenschen* for whom any hope of redemption was forlorn. There was little evidence of newcomers making common cause in the struggle for life. The Protestants and Presbyterians were already halfway to acceptance in the host society by virtue of their religion and cleaved eagerly to the establishment.

Religious animosities flared into violence. In 1834 the Ursuline Convent in Charlestown, Boston was burned to the ground by an anti-Irish-Catholic mob. In Philadelphia, tensions rose between established Irish Presbyterians who had arrived there in the years before the Revolution and the Catholic Irish who began pouring in in the first decades of the nineteenth century. The Catholics stood out from the Anglo-Protestant majority. Their religion, with its Latin, incense and celibate priests, set them apart. So too did their manner. They were noisy and boisterous, white folk in pigmentation only. Their customs were irritating, indeed offensive, to the increasingly bourgeois townspeople. To the Ulster Presbyterians, it must have seemed that the world that they had hoped to escape had followed them to blight their happiness. In 1842 'native Americans', as the English stock inhabitants saw themselves, formed the American Protestant Association and launched a campaign of vilification against Roman Catholics. At the same time, the Catholic Archbishop Francis P. Kenrick antagonized the Protestants further by seeking to have Catholic schoolchildren exempted from having to read from the King James version of the bible.

The sectarian hatred simmering between the Irish gave Philadelphia the dubious distinction of being the site of the first urban riot in the United States. On 3 May 1844, angry Catholics broke up an open-air meeting of Ulster Irish in the Kensington section of Philadelphia. Three days later another meeting ended in a street battle and the death of Patrick Fisher, an Irish Protestant. In the fighting that followed a further three people died. The violence resumed the following day. Six non-Catholics were killed and, in retaliation, a Catholic church, a school run by nuns and a meeting house were burned down. The rioting lasted three days and three nights until quelled by the state militia, and by the end sixteen people had been killed on both sides. Two months later a Protestant mob marched into the Southwark area after a rumour swept the town that the Catholics there were stockpiling weapons in churches. The riots have been cited as an example of an early outrage by the Know Nothing movement, which set itself against immigrants and demanded America for the Americans. Scholars have suggested that while native Americans were involved, the dynamic for the violence was provided by inter-Irish hatreds, citing the fact that German Catholic churches were left untouched.

Middle-class Catholic émigrés were only too aware of the low esteem in which their race and religion were held by the host nation. Some tended to explain it as a reflection of Ireland's poor standing in the eyes of the native Americans as a *de facto* British colony which had, unlike themselves, failed to throw off the yoke of oppression. 'A nation circumstanced as Ireland now is', wrote Charles O'Conor, 'commands no respect from ordinary [Americans] ... To make Irish men, as a class, respectable in the eyes of their fellowmen, Ireland must arise from her present state and become a nation.' Such sentiments prompted the foundation of Friends of Ireland societies to press for Irish emancipation, a development that prefigured the campaigns that would be mounted by later generations of Irish Americans to liberate the old country.

In the first third of the nineteenth century America had established itself as a land of opportunity for Irish Protestants and particularly Presbyterians, who found there land, religious freedom and a host community which shared their values and into whose ranks they could comfortably fit. The same could not be said of the

Catholics, who by the end of the period had overtaken them in numbers. The new life offered more chances than the one they had left behind. But it was still arduous and sometimes dangerous and the attitudes of those established there not markedly different to those of the Protestant Ascendancy they had left behind. Many Catholic émigrés continued to see their departure as a woeful necessity and were stricken by homesickness and despondency, ruing the day they had left home.

But the land they had left behind had nothing to draw them home. The United Irishmen uprisings of 1798 had ended in disaster and savage repression, extinguishing any reasonable hopes that Ireland could be liberated by force of arms. Instead the country had been swallowed up into the Union in 1800 and agitation for Catholic emancipation was making painfully slow progress. Indeed, religious strife was unceasing, with the Catholics stubbornly withstanding the efforts of strident evangelicals to get them to abandon the old faith. The economy swung between brief periods of growth and crushing depressions. Many came to believe that the land was cursed. Between 1816 and 1818 bad weather destroyed the grain and potato crop and 50,000 starved to death or died of typhus and smallpox, their resistance weakened by malnutrition. In 1821 the potato harvest failed in Munster, bringing more deaths from starvation and disease. So it went on, famine, epidemic and tempest. In the 1830s the potato harvest, partly or nationally, failed for eight out of ten years. The lamentations of the peasantry echo down to us from contemporary accounts. Some have a prophetic ring to them as if they sensed that, terrible though the times might be, they were about to get much worse.

Rebels storming a barracks during the 1798 uprising in Ireland.

·7·
LAND OF PROMISE

I N JULY 1845, peasants preparing to harvest their potato fields
noticed, with trepidation, that something strange had happened to
their crops. The leaves and stalks had turned black and crumbled at
a touch. When they dug up the tubers, they discovered that they too
had rotted. Even the healthy-looking potatoes they managed to salvage
quickly turned putrid and inedible. The blight, which struck at between
30 and 40 per cent of the crop that year, was *Phytophthora infestans*, a new
disease in Ireland, which flourished in mild, damp conditions. There was
nothing that could be done about it. Crop failures were nothing new in
Ireland, but the potato blight was to prove relentless, returning every year
for the next five years, leaving no respite for the peasants to recover. In
1846 it destroyed 80 per cent of the pota-
toes planted. It struck with malevolent
swiftness. One day the crop looked
healthy and normal. The next, it was lying
black and dead in the fields. The blight
was less severe in 1847, but fewer potatoes
had been planted. It returned again fiercely
in 1848. In 1849 and throughout the
early 1850s harvests were less than half
their pre-Famine levels.

    The Famine was to kill as many as a
million people through starvation and
related diseases, which swept through the
weakened population and caused 1.8 million people to abandon hope of
being able to survive in their own country and to cross the Irish Sea and the
Atlantic. Emigration was already an established fact of Irish life and would
have continued with or without the Famine. But there can be no doubt that
the Great Hunger created the ghastly dynamic that turned the question of
whether to leave or stay into literally a choice between life and death.

(*Left*) Arrival in the Land of Promise. (Painting by Charles F. Ulrich, 1858–1908)
(*Above*) A peasant contemplates his ruined potato crop.

The scale of devastation wrought by the blight was a consequence of the fact that most Irish people depended on the potato for their basic sustenance. In some ways it appeared a miracle product. It was prolific and nutritious, and provided food for nine months of the year. Individual consumption varied from six to nine pounds a day and the peelings were used to feed the family pig. The heavy reliance that peasant households placed on it in all Ireland except Ulster (where oatmeal was the staple) meant that when disaster struck it was bound to be of epic proportions. The first year was not too bad. The machinery of relief was just able to cope with the crisis. But when the blight returned, the flimsy structures of the state collapsed under the weight and death was everywhere.

There are plenty of terrible accounts of the suffering. Nicholas Cummins, a landlord visiting his estate near Skibereen in west Cork, saw 'famished and ghastly skeletons ... such frightful spectres as no words can describe'. A visitor to the north Midlands 'saw sights that will never wholly leave the eyes that beheld them, cowering wretches almost naked in the savage weather, prowling in turnip fields and endeavouring to grub up roots ... little children ... their limbs fleshless, their faces bloated yet wrinkled and of a pale greenish hue ... who would never grow up, it was too plain, to be men and women'. Captain Robert Forbes, master of an American navy schooner carrying relief supplies to Ireland, was horrified by what he saw in the streets of Cork. 'It was the valley of death and pestilence itself ... hovels crowded with the sick and dying; without floors, without furniture and with patches of dirty straw covered with still dirtier shreds and patches of humanity.'

The potato blight not only caused famine in Ireland but was widespread on the Continent, too. German peasants salvaging what they can of their crop. (Painting by G. Bion, 1852)

Begging for relief. A starving crowd besieges the workhouse in 1846.

When the blight first struck it was not apparent to the authorities that a holocaust was approaching. Even if they had been aware of the dimensions of the tragedy, it is doubtful whether the British governments of the day would have behaved very differently from the way they did. They were locked in a psychological prison of laissez-faire economic theories that made the rights of property and the free workings of the marketplace sacrosanct, a cast of mind which we should have no difficulty recognizing today. Even when these rigid bonds of thinking were broken, the scale of the suffering simply overwhelmed the resources the state had at its disposal. The administration of Sir Robert Peel, prime minister from 1841 to 1846 and a man who knew Ireland from his days as chief secretary for the country, showed some imagination. It established a special relief commission and organized a programme of public works to pay labourers a wage that enabled them to buy imported Indian meal. Food depots were set up and prices fixed with the poorest paying the least, to prevent merchants from capitalizing on the crisis. Those who could not work received food aid. Lord John Russell, who succeeded Peel as prime minister in the middle of 1846, was a sterner economic liberal. He closed food depots except on the west coast, suspended the public works programme and forbade relief committees to sell food at less than the market rate. The importation and distribution of food was put in the hands of speculators and entrepreneurs. The official in charge of Irish relief, Sir Charles Trevelyan, appeared to feel it was better that the Irish peasantry starved than they became habituated to state handouts. A suggestion that people should be paid a dole to allow them to keep working on their land was received by him with incredulous exasperation. It was, he said, a manifestation of the thoroughly upside-down principle that 'the government should be made to support the people instead of the people the government'. His writings suggested that he thought the famine was no bad thing, an example of a just nature at work, visiting a corrective disaster on those who had been

Many families were evicted from their cottages during the Famine, unable to pay their rent.

reproductively profligate. The notion that the peasantry had somehow brought this upon themselves was never far away. As Professor Roy Foster put it, 'there was ... an attitude, often unconcealed, that Irish fecklessness and lack of economy were bringing a retribution that would work out for the best in the end'.

Certainly, charitable reactions seem to have been rare. There were some landlords who reacted with compassion, slaughtering cattle to feed their tenants and using rent income to relieve distress. A Protestant observer, Elizabeth Smith, recorded in her journal that 'It's nonsense to talk of good landords as the rule, they are no such thing, they are only the exception. In my walks about this little locality have I not found evidence against them that would fit me for a witness before the Committee of the House, on the causes of Irish misery?' Religious groups such as the Society of Friends (Quakers) behaved with energy and generosity. Protestant relief associations offered soup, often in return for the recipient abandoning his Catholic faith.

Hopelessness and squalor in Carraroe, County Galway.

By and large, the Famine hit hardest the most exposed elements of Irish society, the landless and the smallest farmers, struggling to scratch a living from poor and overcrowded land in the most populous parts of the country. The combination of famine and the British government's response to it left many of them with a conviction that there was no life to be had in Ireland and that this would remain the case as long as the British ruled there. The Famine had destroyed the means of early marriage and rapid reproduction which had contributed to the population explosion of the late eighteenth and early nineteenth century. Scholars assert that the population had peaked well before the Famine. The fact remains that the figure of 8,175,124 recorded in the census of 1841 was never surpassed thereafter and the demographic curve goes into a rapid slide. Ten years later there were only 6.5 million in the country. In 1871 there were 5.4 million, until the population stabilized at around 4.2 million for the whole island at the foundation of the Free State in 1921.

The government's handling of the crisis left a legacy of hatred towards Britain that was to provide a firm foundation for the building of the republican physical force movement in the years to come, both at home and in America. From the start, it appeared that the British had connived in the disaster, deliberately withholding aid as a means of ridding themselves of the troublesome and rebellious native Irish. Queen Victoria was particularly vilified as the legend grew that she had donated only a few pounds to relieve the famine. The fact that Ireland continued to export cattle, butter, wheat, barley and vegetables, mostly to Britain, throughout the Famine years was never forgotten. The bitterness is evident in the inscription on the granite Celtic cross that stands on Grosse Isle in Canada, a memorial to those who died of disease on the voyages westward in the second and third years of the Famine and whose bodies lie in the mass graves below. Erected by the Ancient Order of Hibernians in 1909 the translation of the Gaelic inscription reads:

> Children of the Gael died in their thousands on this island having fled from the laws of the foreign tyrants and an artificial famine in the years 1847–48. God's loyal blessing upon them. Let this monument be a token to their name and honour from the Gaels of America. God Save Ireland.

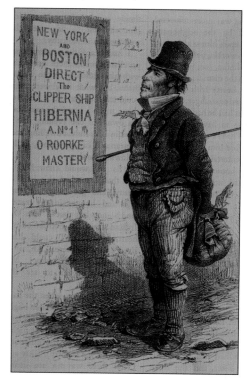

The first step. An Irish farmer contemplates the prospect of a new life in America.

It was to America that the Famine emigrants overwhelmingly chose to go. From 1876 to 1921, some 84 per cent of emigrants went to the United States compared with only 7 per cent to Australia and Canada and 8 per cent to the United Kingdom. It is tempting to see in the preference for America psychological as well as more prosaically economic considerations at work. Emigration to Britain was cheap and, in theory, easily reversible. America, as even the simplest soul making the journey must have known, meant, in all likelihood, exile. The Irish rarely came back, far less so than their Italian, Swedish and Greek counterparts.

As the Famine took hold, what had been an orderly procedure became a headlong rush. Small ships started to set sail for North America from ports all round the Irish coast – from Dublin, Wexford, New Ross, Waterford, Youghal, Cork, Westport, Sligo, Donegal, Londonderry and Belfast. Three-quarters of the Famine exodus would cross the Irish Sea and take passage from Liverpool. A leading historian of the Famine voyages, Edward Laxton, records that 651,931 people arrived on 2,743 voyages during the Famine years. More than half of them landed in New York. Contemporary accounts describe the quays of Dublin thronged with emigrants waiting to board the ships that would carry them into exile. *The Irish Quarterly Review* lamented in 1846:

Preparing to board an emigrant ship to America.

Melancholy, most melancholy is the the sight to the eye, not only of the Dublin citizen or resident, but to the eye of every Irishman who is worthy of being so called and indeed, the spectacle is one of sadness and foreboding. A long continuous procession … a mixed stream of men, women and children, with their humble baggage, who are hurrying to quit for ever their native land!

A look at the passenger list of the *Perseverance*, which set sail for New York on St Patrick's Day 1846, reveals that of the 210 passengers the great majority are described as labourers or servants or without occupation, and there are roughly as many females as males. Laxton calculates that 5,000 vessels made the voyage, of all shapes and sizes and degrees of safety and comfort. Until now the emigrant ships had mainly sailed in the more clement spring and summer months. Now the voyages were year-round. Fares were cheap – an average of two to three pounds to travel steerage to Canada and £3 10s to New York. From Liverpool to Quebec was a journey of 2,625 miles; from Liverpool to New York was 3,043 miles. The voyage took one to two months, depending on winds and weather and the quality of the vessel.

American ships were considered faster, safer and more comfortable. Discrepancies between American and British legislation designed to prevent overcrowding meant that American ships were more spacious, allowing only two passengers per five tons of displacement against the three passengers per five tons on British vessels. Not that the regulations were too rigorously enforced. At the outset of the Famine period captains were supposed to supply their passengers with a pound of food a day made up of bread, biscuit, flour, oatmeal or potatoes, with any other needs being provided by the voyager. Later small supplies of sugar, tea and molasses became obligatory.

Passengers were supposed to receive six pints of water per day to wash with, drink and cook in, but if the voyage was prolonged they would have to make do on reduced rations. They cooked on small, brick-lined hearths, but fires had to be extinguished when the weather was rough. In good weather they were allowed on deck to take the air. But most of the time seems to have been spent below, where the atmosphere may have been fetid but the risk of seasickness was slightly diminished.

There were many perils to alarm the passenger contemplating the voyage, storm and shipwreck among them, but the greatest danger of all was disease. Outbreaks of typhus were particularly prevalent on the Canadian route. No precise figures exist for the number of deaths, but Laxton calculates that in the year 1847 more than 100,000 left for Canadian ports, arriving as early in the spring as the melting ice would permit. The most conservative figures say that, of these 30,000 were infected with typhus, of whom 20,000 died, either at sea or in Quebec and Montreal. In *Passage to America*, a rich account of the transatlantic emigration from Ireland and the United Kingdom the writer Terry Coleman records an emigrant's advice that the best thing that could be done if you contracted typhus was to 'live on until the fever leaves'. This well-meaning counsel was little help against the ravages of the ailment. Typhus affects the blood vessels in the brain and the skin. Its symptoms are shivering, headache, muscular twitching and a vacant look as if the sufferer is intoxicated – the disease's name is derived from the Greek *tuphos* meaning 'mist'. In Irish it was known as *fiabhras dubh*, black fever, from the dark tinge the disease gives to the skin. Medical ignorance of typhus was profound.

Queuing for breakfast on board an emigrant ship.

What was not known was that it was carried in the faeces of lice, which dried to a fine dust. Infection could occur through a cut or even by inhalation. Malnutrition reduced resistance to it. The optimum conditions for its spread were precisely the dirty and overcrowded circumstances that the travellers on the Famine ships found themselves in. Many may already have contracted typhus in Ireland, carrying it with them to Liverpool, for in May 1847 an outbreak of 1,500 cases was reported in the city.

Grosse Isle, an island three miles long and a mile wide, thirty miles east of Quebec on the St Lawrence River, had first been used as a quarantine centre in 1832, after cholera broke out among European emigrants. When it opened again in May 1847, it was under the direction of Dr George Douglas with a staff of one steward, one orderly and one nurse. The wards had room for 200 patients. The first ship to arrive, the barque *Syria* out of Liverpool, had 243 passengers. Nine had died on the voyage and fifty-two were ill. The first victim to die on the island was four-year-old Ellen Keane. Five days later the *Perseverance* and the *Wandsworth* arrived from Dublin. On the *Wandsworth* there had been forty-five deaths. The ships' masters blamed the disease on the fact that their passengers had been starving when they embarked at Dublin and had ravenously consumed the food given them on board. By the end of the month there were 850 patients in the hospital and a further 500 waiting to get in.

Even those who made it off the island were not out of danger. On 8 June with more ships waiting in the river to discharge their disease-ridden human cargoes, Douglas wrote to an official in Quebec warning him of what was coming:

> Of the 4,000 or 5,000 emigrants that have left this island since Sunday, at least 2,000 will fall sick somewhere before three weeks are over. They ought to have accommodation for 2,000 sick at least at Montreal and Quebec, as all the Cork and Liverpool passengers are half dead from starvation and want before embarking and the least bowel complaint, which is sure to come with change of food, finishes them without a struggle. I never saw people so indifferent to life; they would continue in the same berth with a dead person until the seamen or captain dragged out the corpse with boat-hooks.

The first port of call in New York was the Irish Emigrant Society.

Douglas's dedication was heroic. Miraculously, he survived. Forty-four others — doctors, clergymen (Catholic and Protestant), nurses, policemen and servants who carted the corpses away — died.

The voyagers were prolific in recording their experiences. One, gazing over the side, saw 'a shapeless heap move past our ship on the outgoing tide. Presently there was another and another. Another ... caught in our cable and before the swish of the current washed it clear, I caught a glimpse of a white face. I understood it all. The ship in front of us had emigrants and they were throwing overboard their dead.'

Yet a large majority of the migrants fleeing the Famine at this time were heading not for Canada but for the United States and in particular for the city of New York. During the 1840s, for reasons unconnected with the Famine, the port established itself as the premier

point of entry for immigrants from Ireland. New York became an increasingly Irish city and by 1860 there were more than 200,000 Irish-born inhabitants out of a population of about 800,000. Every day for six years, when the Famine exodus was at its height, 300 emigrants would walk down the gangplanks on to the New York quaysides, heading for the nearest lodging houses. If they were lucky, officials of the Irish Emigrant Society, founded in 1841, might be there to advise them on finding jobs and accommodation. Otherwise they were prey to swindlers and conmen, many of them Irish, anxious to relieve them of their luggage and whatever stake money they might have. Many would have arrived with dreams of travelling to the frontier to find farmland or to the goldfields to make their fortunes. Single men and women often moved straight on to dig canals and lay railroads or to join households inland as domestic servants. Some joined family members in established Irish communities in Albany, Buffalo, Rochester or further afield. But, for the bulk of the new arrivals, New York was as far as they got.

Like most immigrants, they tended to huddle together for cultural warmth. Many crossed the East River to Brooklyn, where by 1855 they made up the largest foreign-born group. An enclave around the Navy Yard was dubbed 'Irish Town' and the area retained its strong Irish character well into the following century. In the Bronx they stayed close to the transportation enterprises that gave them employment: the Harlem Railroad, the Hudson River Railroad and the Croton Aqueduct. The poorest settled in shanty towns on the city's edge, or in the barely occupied northern parts of the city in what is now Central Park, living in flimsily built shacks, surrounded by pigs and goats, working as day labourers and scavenging for food.

Railroad workers in Indianola, Utah, 1900. Irishmen helped open up the land to vast transportation networks.

The men worked as dockers, unskilled hands in factories, coachmen, carters and porters and in the construction business as hod-carriers, bricklayers, carpenters and masons. They worked in gangs, almost always with other Irishmen, socializing with each other when the long days were done. Pay was poor. In 1846 Irish labourers in the Brooklyn docks went on strike for 87 cents and a ten hour day. The canal diggers were better off, but not much. Seven years later, Irishmen on the Erie Canal were agitating for $1.25 a day for ten hours' work. Some men showed some entrepreneurial leanings, running small businesses like liquor stores, grocery shops, small hotels and above all saloons.

As well as finding jobs as servants in private homes or hotels, where they could live with their employers and save their wages, Irishwomen were often employed as seamstresses, working in their own homes for contractors. The married ones took in lodgers and washing. Some founded small businesses selling fruit and vegetables, perhaps graduating to ownership of a small grocery store or liquor shop. There was fun to be had. Shocked accounts of the heavily Irish sixth ward in 1850 describe the notorious Five Points area, only a few hundred yards from City Hall, as a warren of taverns, oyster houses and brothels frequented by 'sailors, negroes, and the worst of loafers and vagabonds'. Labour disputes between blacks and Irish could create animosity and violence. In one incident in 1855, Irish stevedores struck for higher wages and were dismissed and replaced by blacks. Fighting broke out and eventually the whites were reinstated. But blacks and Irish seem to have lived in reasonable harmony when economic tensions were low. They sometimes shared the same occupations, as pawnbrokers, rag and junk dealers, hairdressers and waiters. Black and white men and women seem to have habitually drunk, danced and made love together, as Charles Dickens noted with surprise when he visited Peter Williams's tavern in the Five Points during a visit in the early 1840s. Some of them even got married.

Not all the Irish were poor. The community in New York contained more settled immigrants, at the apex of which was a small class of doctors, lawyers and teachers, who formed themselves into charitable organizations like the Emigrant Society and the Friendly Sons of St Patrick to extend a helping hand to the newcomers. A portrait of an entrepreneurial Irishwoman was provided by Jeremiah O'Brien, visiting from Philadelphia in 1854. He encountered a 'Mrs O'Doherty ... a widow, young, handsome, modest ... she is both a milliner and dressmaker and has a house full of young ladies sewing for her'.

There were examples of Irishmen who had prospered in the clothing business, like Patrick Rogers, a native of County Tyrone who owned the six-storey Union Hall men's clothing store or Daniel Devlin from County Donegal who was a pioneer in men's ready-to-wear apparel which he sold from a handsome building on Broadway. For most Irishmen, however, the best chance of advancement lay not in individual enterprise but more modestly with membership of the political client system that provided secure jobs in the building, maintenance and control of what was rapidly becoming one of the great cities of the world. Irish solidarity would have a great impact on urban politics in America, and the Irish were associated with the Democratic party through the alliances between the United Irishmen who fled home after the failure of their uprising and the anti-aristocratic followers of Jefferson and Andrew Jackson, the populist seventh president (1829–37). Catholics naturally inclined towards the Democrats in reaction to the strong anti-Catholic strain found in the opposing parties, the Whigs, Republicans and particularly the Know Nothings. As Hasia R. Diner has pointed out, the Irish influx arrived in New York at a time when a Whig and later Republican rural, upstate legislature was trying to control the affairs of the city. Irish support for the Democrats helped them to dominate the municipal government more or less from the late 1840s on. Thus questions of ethnicity and religion joined other contentious political issues that divided legislature and municipal government. Diner has written that 'the Democrats increasingly articulated a pro-Irish, pro-immigrant position, while the Whig–Republicans owed much of their strength to nativists, in the city and around the state. These battle lines drawn in the 1840s and 1850s played themselves out for decades until the end of the century.'

In return for giving his vote to the Democratic party, the unskilled Irish immigrant male could expect something in return – a job. Large scale municipal construction projects supported many New York Irish families. Irishmen made up most of the payroll in the building of the New York State Supreme Court. By 1855 Irishmen were the largest ethnic group among the cartmen of New York, who worked on sewer-digging, road-building and so on. To be a cartman you needed a licence and to get a licence you needed connections.

The Democratic machine held in its gift positions in the police force at neighbourhood and ward level, and a tradition of Irish policemen was established which remains to this day. By 1855, 27 per cent of the New York police force had been born in Ireland, the same proportion as there were Irish in the population. They received promotion faster than other groups. In 1869 there were no German police captains, even though Germans made up New York's second largest ethnic block, but there were thirty-two from Ireland. The grip of the Irish on the police force

The Irish policeman was ubiquitous. Sergeant O'Hanlon of Danbury, Connecticut.

'The Tiger's Share'. The Tammany Tiger ruled New York.

'Can the law reach him?' 'Boss' Tweed, as seen by satirical cartoonist Thomas Nast in *Harper's Weekly*, 1872.

grew even stronger when the force expanded after the Civil War. Despite this domination there seems to have been little sign of partiality by the cops towards their countrymen, who made up a large proportion of the people they arrested. The Irish policeman served as a symbol of upward mobility and more importantly, of acceptance. The host society, or at least the part of it that was New York, had seen fit to entrust Irishmen, Catholic Irishmen, with responsibility for the enforcement of law. This was a concept that would have seemed unthinkable in the old country at the time when the emigrants had quit its shores.

That said, there was little enthusiasm among the party bosses for allowing Catholic Irishmen too far up the ladder, and between 1845 and 1870 they were generally excluded from elective offices. Professor Miller notes that 'the great mass of Irish Democrats … in New York City had to be content with jobs shovelling dirt in Central Park, with baskets of food in hard winters, with an occasional foot on the lower rungs of the civil service … and with whatever psychic satisfaction came from watching party leaders outrage Protestant propriety'. Irish participation in politics at its most basic level – multiple voting and frightening opposition supporters from the polling booths – did little to dispel the Irish reputation for untrustworthiness and violence.

The attraction of the Democratic party for the Irish was to prove enduring, and it is easy to see why. However cynical the protection offered by the likes of William 'Boss' Tweed, who during the 1860s dominated Tammany Hall, the New York City and state party headquarters, and his Catholic Irish successors John Kelly and Richard Croker, it was a sign to the Catholic Irish that they could be associated with power. It is not too fanciful to speculate that in their relationship with the urban lords of the Democratic party, the immigrants were answering some ancestral folk memory of the days of chieftains and high kings, when loyalty to the mighty was rewarded and there were strong ties of responsibility between ruler and ruled. Certainly the democratic atmosphere of New York, where in the streets at least Jack was as good as his master, delighted simple souls who were used to the haughty manners of their betters back in Ireland. 'People that cuts a great dash at home', wrote Patrick Dunny, an émigré from County Carlow in 1856, 'when they come here the[y] tink it strange for the humble Class of people to get as much respect as themselves [but] when they come here it wont do to say i had such and was such and such at home [for] strangers here the[y] must gain respect by there conduct and not by there tongue'.

The Irish lingered long at the bottom of the urban social pile. By 1880, 20 per cent of all the Irish in the city were designated as 'labourers' in comparison with 4 per cent of native-born Americans. Perhaps their overwhelmingly rural backgrounds fitted them badly for metropolitan life. They lived in the worst housing in the most overcrowded conditions. They suffered the highest rates of typhus, typhoid fever, cholera. They were admitted to lunatic asylums and prisons, charity hospitals and almshouses in greater proportions than any other ethnic group. Irish institutions rapidly grew up to try and answer the pressing social needs of the newcomers. In 1846 the Irish-based Sisters of Mercy were invited to come and minister to homeless, workless Irishwomen in the city.

Behind most of these benevolent institutions stood the Catholic Church. In 1842 John Hughes became Bishop and later Archbishop of New York and for the next twenty-two years he worked to make Catholicism an assertive, even aggressive, force in the city, buttressing his strategy with the manpower supplied by the incoming Irish. He promoted Catholic banks, schools, hospitals and orphanages, in which were nurtured a hybrid culture of Catholic values, Irish nationalism and American patriotism. Irish Catholic churchgoing was not very highly developed, either among the newcomers or among the pre-Famine immigrants. Hughes and his successor John McCloskey built churches and institutions that drew the Irish into intense patterns of observance in which the church became the centre not just of devotional life but of social life as well.

The conditions of urban life reinforced the immigrants' sense of nationality. Union wage struggles against employers reinforced male solidarity, binding workers together with ties of class as well as ethnicity. Newspapers aimed at an Irish audience, easily reached where they were crammed together in the ghettos, with titles like the *Irish World* and the *Irish American*, reinforced identity and enmeshed readers in the political news from the old country. The freedom of the New World allowed immigrants to express their nationality freely and they took full advantage of it with monster parades on St Patrick's Day.

In short, a new national consciousness was burgeoning in the transplanted soil of the Irish exodus. Through the middle years of the century Irish Catholics grew in confidence and boldness, advertising their presence and demanding their rights to a political and social establishment that in many respects remained hostile towards them. At the same time, they sought to use their nascent power externally, as a weapon in the unending struggle with Britain.

Green triumphalism. A St Patrick's Day Parade in the 1870s.

·8·

THE ROAD TO PROSPERITY

VISITING THE UNITED STATES in 1903, Sir James Power, the Lord Mayor of Dublin, wrote that, somewhat against his expectations, the Irishman in America was not 'merely a hewer of wood and a drawer of water'. Poles, Italians, Chinese and blacks now fulfilled that function. Instead, he said, 'Irishmen are universally respected and are found occupying many of the respectable positions in society.' This announcement of the triumph of Ireland Abroad was premature. But there was no doubt that by the turn of the century Irish America was an established fact. Its members had planted themselves squarely at the centre of national life, combating deep-rooted Protestant and nativist prejudice, winning for themselves in the process a fair degree of prosperity and security and a sizeable, not to say disproportionate, influence in the worlds of politics and organized labour. To some extent they were favoured by the times. The Irish propensity for hard, physical work suited a society bursting with capitalist expansionist energy. At the same time high literacy rates (by 1900, 95 per cent of emigrants could read and write in English) made them employable in the proliferating offices and bureaucracies that accompanied industrial expansion.

The Irish had discovered a natural home in metropolitan America. The historian Lawrence J. McCaffrey states that 'urban America was a formidable challenge, but one full of adventure and promise. In it, Irish Americans found a permanent niche as labor leaders, professionals, athletes and entertainers, and as decent, hard-working family men and women. Many had the opportunity to see their daughters and sons rise to heights unthinkable in the Ireland they had left.'

(*Left*) A quay scene at Cobh, near Cork, *c.* 1912. Successive waves of emigration continued into the twentieth century, reinforcing the separateness of Irish America. (*Above*) Moving up: Irish businesses in South Boston, Massachusetts, 1916.

The emergence of an Irish America might not have been possible had it not been for sustained mass migration from the homeland. Without the continued numerical and cultural reinforcement provided by the mainly Catholic newcomers, Irish identity and separateness might have more easily found itself subsumed into America's ethnic broth. As it was, there was no shortage of new blood. After the Famine, conditions in rural Ireland had grown no more conducive to keeping the young at home. A cruel lesson had been learned. What remained of the tradition of partible inheritance vanished. One son inherited the farm and one daughter was granted a dowry. There was no industry to soak up the surplus. The imperial British army and the newly founded Royal Ulster Constabulary provided some males with jobs and even careers. For the women there was domestic or shop work. For both there was always the Church. For many, though, the only real choice lay in the voyage across the Atlantic.

Increasingly, there was money available to make the trip. Throughout the second half of the nineteenth century remittances flowed steadily from North America to Ireland at a rate of £1 million a year, of which 40 per cent was in the form of pre-paid passages. The journey became easier as the century progressed. Since the 1850s, steamships had reduced the passage time from five to two weeks and the vessels were cleaner and more comfortable. The chaos that met the early emigrants when they docked in New York had been replaced by order and discipline. In 1855 the Castle Garden immigration centre opened, providing newly-arrived passengers with bathrooms and kitchens and services for changing money, sending mail and finding accommodation.

Recruiting officers enlisting from the ranks of immigrants at Castle Garden in 1864.

A teeming immigrant quarter of New York City.

Celebrations sometimes turned into riots like this one that erupted on St Patrick's Day in New York in April 1867.

The process of coping with the bewildering world of industrial America, let alone mastering it, was not an easy one. The Irish were being thrust from a primitive, rural society into an aggressively modern environment with no intervening period for acclimatization or familiarization. They brought with them primitive ways. In New York, Irish males formed gangs that replicated the old rural terror societies that had sought to inflict revenge on landlords. In Hell's Kitchen, one of the roughest neighbourhoods, the activities of the Gopher, Gorilla, Parlor and Rhodes gangs made it a no-go area for the police.

Political antagonisms from home flared up into rioting on the streets, notoriously in the Orange Lodge riots of 1870 and 1871 when Catholic workers clashed with Protestants celebrating the Twelfth of July; the result was seventy-six deaths and numerous arrests and injuries. Catholic Irish behaviour outraged native Protestant sensibilities. Professor McCaffrey describes how boys swam in the filthy, sewage-polluted East and Hudson rivers, while their elder brothers and fathers watched men pummel each other in bare-knuckle fights, or bet on cockfights and rat-killing terriers. They lived in appallingly unsanitary conditions in overcrowded, ramshackle tenements on the lower East Side, the middle East Side and the middle West Side. The ghettos stank, of human and animal excrement, and of the noxious outpourings of slaughter houses. Mental illness, schizophrenia and depression, were widespread. So too was alcoholism. The tenements rang to the yells of drunken men and the cries of their beaten wives.

The cartoonist Thomas Nast seized on the St Patrick's Day riot for another of his portrayals of the Irish as violent subhumans.

This wildness contributed to the existing antipathy that native, Protestant America felt towards the Irish on account of their Catholicism. At one level there was a genuine conviction that Gaelic Catholic behaviour and values were incompatible with the sobriety, cleanliness and materialism that underpinned their conceptions of society. In short, Irishmen and women could not make good Americans. The Irish were caricatured in popular plays and literature as Biddy and Paddy, talkative buffoons. Cartoonists, echoing their British counterparts, portrayed the Irishman as a simian drunk, lurching from bar to brawl.

The most visceral manifestation of anti-Irish feeling was found in the activities of the Know Nothing movement and its attendant societies. The name derives from the supposed response when members were asked about their aims: 'I know nothing in our principles which is contrary to our constitution.' The Know Nothings were stridently anti-emigrant. Their refrain was a familiar one. Addressing the Massachusetts State Senate in January 1855, the governor Henry J. Gardner, who supported the movement, declared that nearly four-fifths of beggary, two-thirds of pauperism and three-fifths of crimes sprang from immigrants. America should be for the Americans. Immigration should be controlled. Alien paupers should be returned home. The movement's supporters combined their anti-emigrant animus with a strong anti-Catholicism. In scare-mongering pulp stories such as *The Stolen Nuns* and *The Haunted Convent*, priests were presented as seducers and kidnappers.

Anti-Irish prejudice surfaced in publications like the *American Protestant Magazine* and in the formation of anti-Catholic gangs such as the Order of the American Star, the Wide Awakes, the Black Snakes, the Thunderbolts, the Rip Saws and the Live Oak Club. American born natives fought Irish in street brawls. The North Carolina *Weekly Standard* published a Know Nothing menu: 'Catholic broth; Jesuit soup; Roasted Catholic; Broiled priest, The Pope's Big Toe, broiled; Fried nuns, very nice and tender; (Dessert) Rich Irish Brogue; Sweet German Accent.'

The Know Nothings, who later styled themselves the American Party, were a short-lived phenomenon and by the end of the 1850s had been swept away in the great upheavals that preceded the Civil War. It had been pointed out that, in retrospect, it was inevitable that some nativist anti-immigrant movement would emerge in America. It was equally inevitable that it would fail, for America's success at this period of its life depended on immigration.

If the nativists had had any genuine interest in reforming the manners and attitudes of the Irish immigrants then their antipathy to the Catholic Church was stupid. It was the parish priests of the ghettos who led their flock on the great march towards respectability, responsibility and patriotism. The devotional movement that was flourishing in Ireland under the stern leadership of Cardinal Cullen, who dominated Irish Catholicism until his death in 1878, was equally vigorous in the United States. As we have seen, Archbishops Hughes and McCloskey in New York forced Catholicism to the centre of events. The construction of the magnificent St Patrick's Cathedral on Fifth Avenue could not be a bolder assertion of the Catholic, and particularly the Irish Catholic, place in the life of the city.

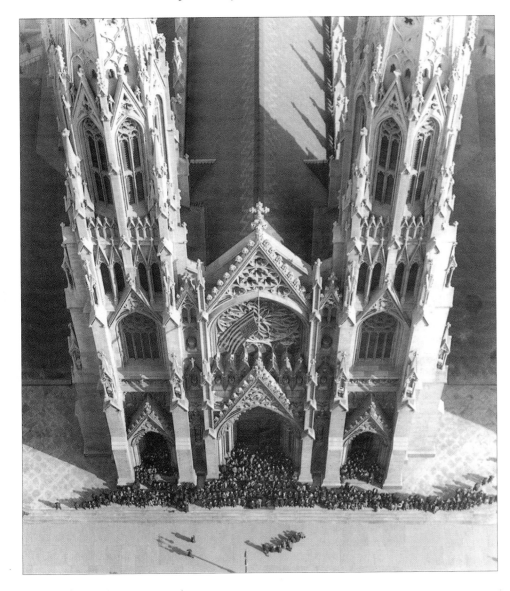

The power and the glory. The grandiose façade of St Patrick's Cathedral, New York.

The contrast with St Patrick's could not be starker. Pilgrims at Knock in the 1860s.

The Church acted as a political focus and a provider of social services that reinforced Irishness while inculcating civic values. Individual parish priests, working in the tradition of the peasant priests of Ireland, sprang from and were revered by their congregations and carried enormous moral authority. Priests not only administered the sacraments but acted as social invigilators, castigating drunken and violent husbands and delinquent children. Male attendance at Mass was high and some headway was made by the temperance movement, following a visit by the indefatigable Fr Theobald Mathew of Cork in 1851. But women were the backbone of the congregations. In many households women provided a discipline and practised a continence that their menfolk lacked, managing domestic life and providing a moral lead for the children.

An innate conservatism chimed with the message from the pulpits. Irish Catholicism, while still loyal to notions of independence for the homeland, remained suspicious of socialistic trends and hostile to any politics which threatened to challenge the essential tenets of American society. The successor to Cardinal McCloskey (as he became) in New York, Archbishop Michael Augustine Corrigan, established a tradition of conservatism and authoritarianism which made him a cold, remote figure. Corrigan had no interest in efforts to attack the root causes of the poverty that afflicted so many of his flock. Indeed he believed that poverty was part of the natural order and that those who endured it would have their reward in the next life. Thus he was opposed to unions and regarded reform movements as the vanguard of secular materialism. Corrigan maintained a fierce, ultramontane loyalty and his views were in keeping with the papal conservatism of the time. His successor, the Irish-born John M. Farley, was also conservative but a less chilly personality, willing to tolerate and even encourage the airing of new ideas. A seminary, St Joseph's at Dunwoodie in Yonkers, became a centre for modernizing thought which opposed itself to the view that contemporary events should be a matter of indifference to a Church founded on verities that remained unaffected by the passage of time. But Farley accepted the discipline of a 1907 encyclical by Pius X condemning modernism, orthodoxy was imposed and the leading voices of the new thinking were removed from the seminary.

Cardinal McCloskey.

If the Church was one pillar that supported the building of an Irish identity inside the United States, the other was politics. As the nineteenth century progressed, the Irish established a grip on the Democratic machine in many towns and cities outside the Deep South and in particular in New York. There was ingrained opposition to Irish advancement from nativists. In 1870 the New Jersey state legislature abolished elective government in Jersey City after Irish Catholics were elected to municipal office. In 1885 Boston's police force was removed by the Massachusetts legislature from city control after Hugh O'Brien became the first Irish mayor.

The fall of Boss Tweed in 1871 opened the way for the Irish to reach the top of Tammany Hall. He was replaced by 'Honest' John Kelly, who pledged to clean the overflowing Augean stables left by Tweed. But a comprehensive reform would have destroyed the patronage system of support and reward that created a symbiotic relationship between the Irish and Tammany Hall. Kelly was careful to distinguish between 'honest' graft, where the benefit was due to services rendered, and 'dishonest' – that is, straightforward theft. His successor was less scrupulous. Richard Croker, who took over in 1886, had left Ireland during the Famine at the age of three, and started his Democratic party career as a street thug. His scandalous manipulation of power and wholesale corruption eventually forced him out. He retired to the old country, where he bred horses and luxuriated in his status as a supreme example of the rich, returned 'Yank'. Charles Francis Murphy, who took over Tammany in 1902, was a hard-working, conscientious, dour political fixer who schooled a younger generation of Irish American politicians in the workings of the machine. Murphy developed an ideological edge to his politics, believing in the duty of government to intervene. But at the end of the day the Tammany system was a crude affair, a sort of urban, capitalist feudalism which spoke the language of universalism but which felt its first duty was towards its own. To the Irish went the spoils. The rest had to be content with what small largesse trickled down to them.

Ethnic considerations also predominated in labour politics, where the Irish had established themselves as truculent, determined and resourceful in their dealings with the bosses. Irish dockers united to exclude blacks, and Irish-led unions would show hostility to non-whites and to newer immigrants. The Irish brought to union activity a tradition, sometimes violent, of rural protest. In the coal mines of Pennsylvania Irish migrants transplanted or re-established the Molly Maguires, a secret society that had spread terror in South Ulster in the late eighteenth century. Overseers at the mines were singled out for murder and mutilation and mine property was destroyed and dynamited. Suspected informants mysteriously disappeared. The activities of the Mollies reached a wider audience during the Civil War, when in 1863 President Lincoln enacted a law conscripting men to the Union forces. Exemption could be bought by a payment of $300. The miners resisted,

Charles Murphy with Franklin D. Roosevelt.

Another Nast illustration, this time portraying the reconstruction of the southern states after the Civil War as a conspiracy between the Irish, the defeated Confederates and rich businessmen to keep down black Union veterans.

rallying under the slogan 'a rich man's war but a poor man's fight'. The need for coal to keep the Union war machine working tempered the authority's reaction to the resistance. Later, another series of murders brought a crackdown and twenty miners were hanged. The attitude of the miners of Pennsylvania towards the war seems typical of Irish working-class opinion towards the conflict. No ideological chords seem to have been struck. Although 200,000 Irishmen were to serve in the war, mainly on the Union side, they seem to have done so out of necessity rather than conviction. Some Irishmen were lured to arms by the promise of a bounty; as much as $700 was on offer, a massive sum for those days.

Ideology, then, did not seem to figure large in the attitude of the Irish towards their new home. They appeared to show a remarkable degree of sophistication in their attitude, having little difficulty combining a stubborn attachment to their Irishness and Catholicism with a love of their adopted country. They also seem to have been able to accommodate an aggressive attitude towards the employing classes with a desire to emulate them and join them. Above all, they were able to distinguish between the *idea* of America and the practical, sometimes disagreeable reality. The attitude is summed up in the exhortation Lawrence McCaffrey heard from his father: 'You know I love Ireland, but never forget that America is the greatest country in the world.'

Where Irishmen did allow themselves to express an ideology it was on the subject of the politics of the homeland. Harsh anti-British attitudes combined with a continuing interest in the progress of the Catholic cause – or lack of it – which was reported in the pages of the Irish American press. Irish proponents of physical force saw in America a reservoir of manpower and funds offering a potential for political agitation beyond the reach of the British authorities. It was, according to one revolutionary leader, John Mitchel, 'the lever that shall move the world'. In 1858 John O'Mahoney and Michael Doheny founded the Fenian Brotherhood. The name was derived from *fianna*, the warrior band of the legendary Irish Gaelic king, Finn MacCool. Both were exiled veterans of the Young Ireland uprising of 1848, another attempt by revolutionary nationalists to throw off British rule, which had ended in miserable failure. O'Mahoney had in 1856 expressed disillusionment with the gap between the rhetoric of his countrymen abroad and their appetite for real action. 'I am sick of Irish Catholics in America,' he wrote. 'I am sick of Yankee-doodle twaddle, Yankee-doodle selfishness and all Yankee-doodle dum!' Nonetheless he worked hard at trying to establish an organization to supply money, arms and trained soldiers for a rebellion to drive the British from Ireland. The Civil War provided the movement with a potential recruiting base among the ranks of Irishmen who had been hardened in the battles of a conflict that was offering a bitter taste of how modern wars would be fought. James Stephens, the founder of the Irish Republican Brotherhood, the Irish branch of the movement, toured the Union armies seeking recruits, and by the end of the war the Brotherhood had 50,000 members. This was an impressive achievement.

But the Fenian movement quickly slithered into disarray. Its aims were grandiose and borne up by wishful thinking, such as the notion that America was prepared to go to war with Britain or at least support the Fenian campaign as a reward for Irish services rendered during the Civil War. In 1865 Stephens was forced to flee Ireland.

The Fenian emblem showing a portrait of the Irish patriot Robert Emmet.

The American movement split and a strategy was adopted of attacking the British Empire at its most accessible point: Canada. On the morning of 2 June 1866 a group of armed men joined battle with a small band of militiamen at Ridgeway, just inside the Canadian border. The Canadians, mostly student volunteers, lost twelve dead and fourteen wounded, the Fenians eight dead and twenty wounded. It is worth noting that the green flag they carried before them that day was adorned with the gold harp of Ireland and the letters 'IRA', the first recorded appearance of the acronym. At the funeral later of Sergeant John Lynch, who succumbed to wounds sustained during this pointless and inglorious encounter, the priest refused to pray over the coffin unless the accompanying 'Finini' removed their uniforms. Irish American officers crossed the Atlantic to take part in an abortive IRB uprising in early 1867. But the failure of the enterprise, combined with the hostility of the Grant government and the factional strife inside the organization, meant that by 1870 American Fenianism had almost died out.

The Fenian leaders periodically complained of the insubstantial nature of Irish American nationalism, which Stephens said consisted of 'speeches of bayonets, gala days and jolly nights, banner and sashes'. Their estimate of what they could hope for from the American Irish was distorted by over-optimism and their own zealous perspective, which took little account of material factors. O'Mahony, Doheny, Stephens and John Mitchel (the son of an Ulster Protestant minister) were men of education who had turned their backs on comfort or advancement for the sake of the cause. That their idealism was not shared by their Irish American countrymen should not have surprised them. But unwillingness to engage in sacrificial military operations did not mean that there was any lack of support for the continuing struggle against landlord oppression at home.

Irish Regiment recruitment poster.

Members of the Irish Brigade of the Union Army.

As the century progressed, the land issue remained as acute as ever. Out of the Fenian defeat a new strategy emerged which combined parliamentary action with mass agitation and the threat of violence, in support of demands for land reform and self-government. The movement was called New Departure, and among its key figures were John Devoy in America and Michael Davitt in Ireland, both of whom had been imprisoned for their Fenian activities. Davitt had much in his personal history to fuel his opposition to the British. His father had been evicted from his Mayo farm after the Famine, and he himself had lost his right arm in a Lancashire mill at the age of eleven. He joined the Fenians in 1865 and became organizing secretary of the IRB. After serving seven years' penal servitude for sending firearms to Ireland he went to America in 1877, where he teamed up with Devoy, who sent him back to Ireland to mobilize farmers into the National Land League, founded in 1879.

A short-lived spell of prosperity in Ireland came to an end as the 1870s closed. The harvest of 1879 was disastrous and brought severe distress to the rural population, especially in the west. There were fears of another famine. The passivity that marked the peasant reaction to the Great Hunger had disappeared. In its place was a determination not to let history repeat itself, which provided the motor force for the activities of the Land League. The style of the League was partly borrowed from the agitation techniques of Daniel O'Connell, whose campaigning in the 1820s had won Catholic emancipation, with mass meetings and brass bands. In addition, though, the League pioneered techniques of social pressure that were refined forms of some of the tactics employed by the agrarian secret societies. Estates with a reputation for rack-renting and eviction were selected and subjected to the attentions of mass meetings. Rents were withheld, farms from which the tenants had been evicted were kept empty and offending landlords were ostracized and excluded from all transactions within the community, a practice that became known as boycotting. More primitive methods of persuasion were also used: cattle maiming, the firing of warning shots and even murder. The League was a success. In 1882 Gladstone's Liberal government conceded fixed tenures at fair rents. The so-called Land War flared back into life later in the decade, but a major step had been taken on the road to resolving an explosive issue. Irish Americans played a vital part in the campaign, particularly through fund raising. It was often said that the financial engine powering the League was the pennies of Irish servant girls toiling in America.

The voice of Irish nationalism, often revolutionary in tone, was loudly represented in America through Clann na Gael, which replaced the Fenian movement. Under Devoy's direction, the organization steered a course of its own, resenting the Democrats' assumption that the Irish vote belonged to them exclusively. Devoy urged his followers to vote for whichever candidate was most pro-nationalist, regardless of party, and in 1884 he and his associates endorsed Republican presidential candidates.

Their concentration on the Irish question meant that nationalist radicals had a limited appeal for voters preoccupied with more day-to-day concerns, and they lost out to politicians and parties who associated themselves with the more prosaic requirements of the Irish electorate. The pattern, established by the Land League, was maintained, however. America provided a treasure chest for Irish nationalism and a stream of individuals for the cause. But geographical and socio-political considerations meant that the support that nationalists could expect from that quarter was limited. As Irish America established itself, its anti-Britishness seemed to take on a formulaic quality. Close attention to the detail of the political question of the day slackened and attitudes were overlaid with a fuzzy, all-purpose hostility to 'British oppression'. This process reached its nadir in Irish American attitudes to the resurgence of the Northern Ireland troubles in the early 1970s. Journalists seeking the opinions of Irish Americans, even those actively involved in nationalist organizations, were surprised to hear that they believed that Catholics in Northern Ireland did not have the vote.

If revolutionary nationalism was to prosper in America, it needed Irishmen and women to regard themselve as exiles. By the end of the nineteenth century, this was no longer the case. Catholic emigration gradually came to lose its associations of alienation and loss and, as with the Protestant exodus before it, to acquire connotations of adventure and opportunity. One small but symbolically important indication of the trend was the altered nature of the 'wake' that traditionally accompanied departure overseas. As time went on, the occasion lost its tragic overtones and became more in the nature of a celebration. In Connaught it became known as the 'farewell supper' or 'feast of departure', in Donegal the 'American bottle night', and in Meath and Wexford the 'parting spree'.

A woman's lot in rural Ireland. Cutting the peat in County Cork.

Emigration was to become less involuntary. Despite what could be seen as an overall net improvement in the economic and political circumstances of Irish Catholics, the exodus continued, particularly to America. By 1870 more than half as many natives of Ireland were living overseas as at home and up to half of each generation was choosing to live abroad. Three-fifths of the emigrants were living in the United States, a quarter in Britain, with the rest in Australia, New Zealand and Canada. In each boat you were likely to find as many women as men. In some years the lack of opportunities at home combined with a wealth of openings abroad to produce a majority of female emigrants.

For women in particular, emigration equalled opportunity. The status of females was low in rural Ireland and it sank lower after the Famine. They were expected to labour in the fields as well as to carry out traditional and heavy 'women's work' such as churning butter, which the men disdained. Confinements were frequent and child-rearing constant. At table, women commonly started to eat only when the men had had their fill. They lived shorter lives than their sisters in Britain and America. Marriages were arranged, and were often matches between total strangers. Unmarried women were totally under the authority of their fathers and brothers and were expected to be chaste, or scandal would fall on them and the family and they would lose their value in the marriage market. The Church taught a doctrine of subordination and docility. Brutality and neglect at the hands of bad husbands were a cross to bear, to be 'offered up' as a penance.

In these circumstances, escape from the stifling life of rural conservatism must have seemed attractive to a young woman of spirit. The primary impulse to emigrate, though, was economic. There were few jobs to be had outside the ranks of domestic service, an occupation whose status was so low that it was to be considered only as a last resort. Overseas, the job carried no such stigma. Letters home presented a picture of well-paid work in comfortable surroundings and the intoxicating prospect of a degree of personal liberty. Thomas McCann wrote of his emigrant sister that 'Maggie is well and likes this country. She would not go back to old Ireland for any money.' Mary Brown reported that she thought America 'the loveliest place on earth'.

For many of the women, America offered the chance of finding a husband of one's own choice. Emigration meant that men were in short supply, and those who were available tended to be elder sons, leading to a widening gap in the age differences between spouses. In America there were plenty of men, and letters home described the wealth of suitors a young woman could expect in the land of 'love and liberty'.

The picture of prosperity and freedom was at odds with the reality endured by women working in the mill towns and factories of the eastern seaboard states. In towns like Lawrence, Massachusetts, where the population was 65 per cent Irish, women had to contend with seasonal unemployment, low wages and high accident rates. They responded collectively, agitating against poor pay and conditions. In 1882 women working at the Pacific Main mill, the town's biggest employer, went on strike when wages were cut. Irishwomen became active in the labour movement of the late nineteenth century and some of them gained prominent positions. Among them was Mary Harris 'Mother' Jones, who was a familiar figure at labour disputes throughout her long life. Clarence Darrow, the liberal lawyer, wrote in his introduc-

Factory life in the US. Women workers pose in front of the spinning frames at a mill in Lawrence, Massachusetts, c. 1911.

tion to her autobiography that she was a 'born crusader, a woman of action, fired by a fine zeal, a mother especially devoted to the miners. Wherever the fights were fiercest and danger greatest, Mother Jones was present to aid and cheer ... Her personal non-violent resistance was far more powerful than any appeal to force.'

Mary Harris (née Jones) had come to the United States as a five year old in 1835 and was brought up in Toronto. She started her own dressmaking business and ended up teaching in Memphis, Tennessee, where in 1861 she met and married her husband. He died six years later, along with the couple's four children, when a Yellow Fever epidemic swept through Memphis. She moved to Chicago, but lost everything in the great fire of 1871. She became interested in labour issues and began attending meetings of the Knights of Labor, an early workers' organization, later travelling round the country speaking in support of strikers, particularly miners. She had a keen awareness of the value of publicity, on one occasion leading a procession of children into New York to draw attention to the abuse of child labour, one of her many causes. She was jailed several times and was once convicted, on a trumped-up charge of conspiracy to commit murder. She was still active in her nineties, died aged 100 and was buried in the Miners' Union cemetery in Mt Olive, Illinois. The priest who delivered the eulogy declared that 'wealthy coal operators and capitalists throughout the United States are breathing sighs of relief while toil-worn men and women are weeping tears of bitter grief. The reason for this contrast of relief and sorrow is apparent. Mother Jones is dead.'

The adversity and danger which accompanied industrial life at the bottom seemed to have a galvanizing effect on Irishwomen like Leonora Barry, who started work in a hosiery mill when widowed and became a full time organizer for the Knights of Labor, and Mary Keeney O'Sullivan, who worked in a book bindery when her father was killed in an industrial accident.

Mill work was hard and conditions were dreadful. Child labour was widely used. In Lawrence in 1912, half the children aged between fourteen and eighteen worked in mills and one in ten textile workers was under eighteen. Lawrence was the most congested city in America, with the highest infant mortality rate, and 36 per cent of the men and women employed in the factories died before they were twenty-five. The Great Lawrence strike of 1912 become known as the 'Bread and Roses' strike after a placard brandished by one woman which read: 'We Want Bread and Roses Too'. The slogan inspired a classic song of struggle:

> As we come marching, marching
> In the beauty of the day
> A million darkened kitchens
> A thousand mill lofts grey
> Are touched with all the radiance
> That a sudden sun discloses
> For people hear us singing
> Bread and Roses! Bread and Roses!

The slogan had a political point. It was a jibe at the American Federation of Labor, the largest union at the time, which declared itself to be a 'bread and butter' union limiting its aims to securing basic wages. The women wanted more: better conditions, health care

and facilities for their children – in short a better life. The AFL was reluctant to organize the mill workers, partly on account of the difficulties posed by the plethora of twenty-five different nationalities working in the Lawrence mills. After the strike broke out on 11 January, the revolutionary labour organization, the International Workers of the World, better known as the Wobblies, moved in. The action was triggered by a decision to cut wages in line with legislation requiring employers to limit the hours worked by those aged under eighteen. Among the Wobbly leaders was Elizabeth Gurley Flynn, the descendant, as she proudly said, of 'immigrants and revolutionaries from the Emerald Isle'. A reporter in the crowd at a strike rally described how when she spoke:

the excitement of the crowd became a visible thing. She stood there, young, with her Irish blue eyes, her face magnolia white and her cloud of black hair, the picture of a youthful revolutionary girl leader. She stirred them, lifted them up in her appeal for solidarity. Then at the end of the meeting they sang. It was as though a spurt of flame had gone through the audience; something stirring and powerful, a feeling which has made the liberation of people possible, something beautiful and strong had swept through the people and welded them together, singing.

Elizabeth Gurley Flynn galvanizing a crowd of strikers at a silk mill in New Jersey, 1913.

Ardis Cameron, in her book *Radicals of the Worst Sort*, has described the long, bitter and violent course of the strike. Police and the local militia were brought in to suppress the strikers who were picketing the mills. The strikers sent their children away to be cared for by sympathetic families in New York and Philadelphia. One infamous episode in the evacuation was recorded by Elizabeth Gurley Flynn: 'Just as they were about to board the train they were surrounded by police. Troopers surrounded the station to keep the others out. Children were clubbed and torn away from their parents and a wild scene of brutal disorder took place. Thirty-five frantic women and children were thrown screaming and fighting into patrol wagons. They were beaten into submission and taken to the police station.' The incident caused an outcry that prompted a congressional inquiry in Washington. The Lawrence strike triggered a chain of protests across New England in 1912 and 1913 in what was to be the most widespread labour revolt in American history. The campaign brought about the end of child labour and eventually the adoption of the eight-hour day.

These were the last battles in a war that elsewhere the Irish had almost won. At the turn of the century, looking at some key indices of success, they could congratulate themselves on having hauled themselves alongside native-born, white Americans. By the early years of the new century a higher proportion of Irish American youths were attending college than were children of WASP parentage. Irishmen were employed in roughly the same proportions as their nativist counterparts, that is with 35 per cent of workers in white collar or farming jobs, 50 per cent in skilled occupations and 15 per cent in unskilled employment. The children of immigrants made the passage from labourer to bureaucrat. In Boston in 1890, 40 per cent of second generation Irish held white-collar jobs.

With betterment came aspirations to gentility. The lower-middle classes put up lace curtains and bought a piano for the parlour of their suburban homes to which they had escaped from the tenements and shanties of the inner cities. These upwardly mobile ambitions were welcomed by the native American ruling class as a sign that their fears that the Irish would form a perpetual source of trouble and subversion might be unfounded. In 1896 the *Atlantic Monthly* was writing that the 'Irish will, before many years are past, be lost in the American and … there will be no longer an "Irish question" or an "Irish vote", but a people one in feelings, and practically one in race.' Professor Miller has noted that a graphic symbol of Irish American acceptance in the years 1870–1921 was their changing cartoon caricature 'from Thomas Nast's brutal, half-simian Fenian, to George MacManus's comic portrayal of "Maggie and Jiggs", vulgar but harmless lace-curtain Irish striving for respectability'.

Irish acceptance was accelerated by the growing prominence of Irish performers in the boxing ring and on the sports field and the stage. The Brooklyn Dodgers baseball team which won the National League pennant in 1890 was managed by Bill McGunnigle and had players with names like Collins, Burns, O'Brien, Corkhill and Daly. Lawrence McCaffrey has observed, however, that while baseball prowess may have made the Irish more acceptable, 'athleticism also reinforced native opinion that the Irish were strong of back but weak of mind'. Irish performers appeared in theatres and vaudeville revues, and dramatic representations of Irishmen and women became increasingly warm and affectionate. It was the age of sentimental ballads idealizing a remote, rural idyll, such as 'When Irish Eyes Are Smiling' and 'Mother Machree'. In the world of vaudeville, the main form of American popular entertainment from 1875 to the advent of the radio age in 1925, the most influential writer and performer was an Irish American, George M. Cohan. The son of vaudevillians, together with his writing partner Sam Harris he transformed the genre with all-singing, all-dancing displays which combined good humour with an overpowering patriotism exemplified by 'Yankee Doodle Dandy'.

The entertainer George M. Cohan in patriotic pose, playing FDR.

By the early twentieth century, then, the Irish had created an identity for themselves that was dramatically at odds with the image that had attached to them a hundred years previously. Some prejudices would linger, but by and large they were judged to be good citizens and to display qualities that endorsed or supplemented values that older-established Americans prized. They were brave, humorous, friendly and co-operative and they were good sons and daughters. Their gregariousness and sociability perhaps added a welcome extra facet to the American character to complement the rugged individualism of the frontier tradition. It was a reputation that was to enable the Irish to establish themselves at the very heart of American life in the new century.

· 9 ·

APART IN BRITAIN

EMIGRATION TO AMERICA was an epic experience, as dramatic and fateful in the terms of the times as a voyage to another planet would be today. Journeying to Britain, by contrast, was a much more familiar proposition. There had always been strong economic and social ties between the two islands, a constant toing and froing of trade, migrant workers, harvesters, labourers and young men off to take the king's or queen's shilling in Britain's army and navy. The journey was cheap; a few pence to travel on the deck of the vessels plying between Ireland and English, Welsh and Scottish ports. As we have seen, the Irish were a regular if not particularly welcome feature in the consciousness of the authorities, popping up as vagrants, beggars, paupers and quarrelsome soldiers of fortune. In literature they appear in a more amiable light, as good servants, especially grooms and gardeners.

From the beginning of the fifth century, as we have seen, Irish raiders took advantage of the vacuum created by the collapse of Roman power to settle along the western seaboard of England and Wales and later founded the kingdom of Dal Riata in Scotland. By the Middle Ages there were recognizably Irish quarters of British cities. In Bristol, the leading trading port with Cork and southern Ireland, the Irish community is said to have protested during Cromwell's time at the public auction of Irishwomen and children who, it was claimed, were exposed naked in the cattle market for inspection and purchase by agents of the planters of Virginia and the West Indies. Liverpool's proximity made it another place of settlement and by the seventeenth century 1,800 manual labourers were reckoned to live there. But

(*Left*) An Irish emigrant arriving at Liverpool in 1871. (Painting by Erskine Nicol, 1824–1904) (*Above*) Irish farm labourers at Holyhead Pier jostle to board the Dublin packet to return home after a season of harvest work in England, 1825.

Harvest celebration in Leitrim, 1892.

long before the big migrations of the nineteenth and twentieth centuries a sprinkling of Irish could be found in many corners of Britain – such as Canterbury, Norwich, London and York, drawn by work or circumstances that now elude discovery.

The relative ease of movement meant that emigration to Britain was probably usually conceived of as a temporary measure. Home was just over the water and return was always possible. Much of the work that attracted the emigrants was seasonal, dictated by harvest timetables. The army and navy worked to longer rhythms. By the end of the eighteenth century, though, the pattern starts to change. Seasonal workers and vagrants began to stay on, compelled by the lack of opportunity back home. The same economic hardship, compounded by the religious and political conflict, impelled others to join them from Ireland. At the start of the nineteenth century the numbers of Irish in the big mainland cities started to boom. In Glasgow, estimates of the number of Irish Catholics rose from 8,245 in 1819 to 25,000 in 1821 and 31,000 in 1831. There were believed to be 100,000 Irish in Lancashire in 1825, 35,000 of them in Manchester and 24,000 in Liverpool. The British army and navy provided another sort of haven. It has been calculated that in 1830 the Irish accounted for an astonishing 42 per cent of the non-commissioned ranks of the army.

By the time of the census of 1841, when Irish immigrants were officially recorded for the first time, there were more than 400,000 in England, Scotland and Wales, representing 1.8 per cent of the population of England and Wales and 4.8 per cent of the population of Scotland. Ten years later, boosted by the Famine, the numbers had risen again, reaching what proved to be the high-water mark of the Irish as a proportion of the mainland population – 2.9 per cent in England and Wales and 7.2 per cent in Scotland.

The emigrants of the post-Famine years were in many cases desperate and hungry as they flooded the western ports of England and Scotland. In 1846 more than 280,000 arrived in Liverpool. Many, maybe most, had ambitions to move on to

America, but probably less than half of them succeeded. The following year another 300,000 turned up, and again many of them, particularly the poorest, stayed on. In Glasgow in the same year, 26,000 poured in in two months. We can gauge the condition of many of the immigrants from the records of the Asylum for the Homeless Poor in Cripplegate, London which show that in the years 1834–5 only 300 Irish were admitted. In 1846–7, the number leaps to 7,576 and in 1847–8 to 10,756.

A painting executed in 1853–4 by the Pre-Raphaelite Walter Howell Deverell called *The Irish Emigrants* shows what must have been a reasonably authentic scene of the time. A group of paupers is slumped at the side of the road. One man is asleep, another sunk in depression. An infant sleeps on the breast of its dazed mother. Two half-naked children plead for alms from a haughty woman who rides by without pity. The compassion of the Christian Socialist artist was by no means a common reaction. The Irish faced hostility and prejudice at all levels of society, as we shall see later.

Those who escaped from destitution found work in the lowest and worst-paid occupations, herded together in the meanest parts of Britain's growing industrial cities. The immigrant Irish were disproportionately concentrated in the ranks of the unskilled and semi-skilled labour force. The women, like their transatlantic sisters, worked in domestic service or textile mills, the men as building labourers and dockers, above all as navvies, cutting the railways and canals now crisscrossing the country. The term 'navvy' is short for navigator, because in the early, relatively unscientific days

In the nineteenth century, Britain's colonial-style exploitation of Ireland was obvious to contemporaries.

The pick and shovel brigade.

of civil engineering it was often left to the excavators to steer or navigate the true and level course of the path they were cutting. The Irish provided a hardworking and malleable labour force, willing to move from place to place following the work, undeterred by the dirty, backbreaking nature of the labour. Soon they were a familiar sight around the countryside. A witness to the Select Committee on Emigration declared in 1828 that in the construction of any major road, canal or drain he should 'not feel in the least surprised to find, that of a hundred men employed in it, ninety were Irish'.

The difficult and dangerous work undertaken by the navvies' superior skills – they had responsibility for handling the dynamite that blasted the tunnels, for example – meant they could demand higher wages. They worked together in 'butty' gangs of a dozen men lifting huge amounts of dirt, rock and clay. As John Archer Jackson observes in his pioneering study of the Irish in Britain, 'it is difficult to imagine today the immensity of labour involved in the construction of the canals and railways ... Without the advantages of the mechanical drill, bulldozer, mechanical shoveller and tunneller which perform herculean tasks today, an army of labourers, many of them Irish, worked with immense effort and at great risk to rapidly develop a system of communication that proved indispensable to industrial expansion.'

Thomas Brassey, who engineered some of the great projects of the time, recorded that 'each man has to lift nearly twenty tons of earth on a shovel over his head into a wagon. The height of lifting is about six feet ... Some men will accomplish that astonishing quantity of work by three or four in the afternoon, a result I believe not nearly equalled by any other set of workmen in the world.'

Below stairs in Victorian Britain.

Away from the diggings the navvies were boisterous, as *The Navigator's Song* acknowledges:

East End alley, London.

> The canals and the bridges, the embankments and cuts
> They blasted and dug with their sweat and their guts
> They never drank water but whisky in pints
> And the shanty towns rang with their songs and their fights

The navvies formed a sort of heroic vanguard in the war against nature that was a vital part of the industrial revolution. But, despite their high wages and their good internal organization, their rootlessness meant that they rarely established a base from where they could prosper and integrate.

For most of the Irish, life was often dreadfully hard. Jackson notes that 'the Irishman who fled from starvation, eviction and poverty found all too often that he had exchanged his rags and tatters for a bed of sores in the foetid stench of a cramped and overcrowded cellar in Manchester, St Giles or Glasgow'. As the scholar Gerald O'Tuathaigh observes:

> their living conditions were generally the very worst which the Victorian
> industrial slum could offer. The Little Ireland ghetto in Manchester, the London
> courts and rookeries, the Glasgow tenements, the Liverpool cellars – all displayed
> the full spectrum of social evils: appalling overcrowding, little or no sanitation,
> open sewers and cesspools, unhealthy diet, inadequate clothing, vagrancy, disease,
> alcoholism and general squalor, a high quota of unemployed paupers or of
> underemployed casual labourers, and a high incidence of casual violence.

The conditions the Irish lived in shocked contemporaries, whether high-minded reformers or social voyeurs revelling in the foulness they witnessed. The literature of the time is full of descriptions of the degradation in which the immigrants were sunk. One visitor to a Glasgow tenement described seeing several women huddling naked under a blanket in the middle of the day because 'others … had on their backs all the articles of dress that belonged to the party'.

Many were struck by the Irish habit of keeping chickens, goats and above all pigs in their slum homes. Frederick Engels on his tour of England famously reported that 'The Irishman loves his pig as the Arab his horse … he eats and sleeps with it, his children play with it, ride upon it, roll in the dirt with it, as anyone may see a thousand times repeated in all the great towns of England.' The mortality rates that such conditions of life established are almost unbelievable by contempary standards, particularly among children. In Liverpool in 1840, for example, 62 per cent of deaths were of under fives.

A literary picture of the slums into which the immigrant Irish were falling was given by Charles Dickens describing conditions in Saffron Hill, which bordered the infamous St Giles Rookery, in *Oliver Twist*.

A dirtier and more wretched place he had never seen. The street was very narrow and muddy and the air was impregnated with filthy odours … the sole places that seemed to prosper amid the general blight of the place were the public houses, and in them the lowest orders of the Irish were wrangling with might and main. Covered ways and yards which here and there diverged from the main street, disclosed little knots of houses, where drunken men and women were positively wallowing in filth, and from several of the doorways great ill-looking fellows were cautiously emerging, bound to all appearance on no very well disposed or harmless errands.

Dickens's tone was typical of that of the Victorian observer of the Irish poor. The humane gloss that usually attaches to his observations of poverty is missing. The reader is nudged towards the conclusion that the Irish are somehow responsible for their own plight. There is some evidence that the rural background of most of the Irish may have made them especially ill-fitted for the ordeal of slum life. But the truth seems to be that the conditions they lived in were not markedly worse than those endured by the rest of the urban poor. The separateness of the Irish, their peculiarities of speech and custom, marked them out for particular disapproval. Thus, in Victorian eyes, they were deemed dirtier, lazier, drunker and more criminally inclined than their English proletarian counterparts.

Drink was undoubtedly a major cause of disorder in the slums as men and women sought escape from their surroundings in the bottle, and it would be vain to deny that a reputation for brawling may have been deserved. A publican insisted that he would 'rather have twenty poor Englishmen drunk in my tap-room than a couple of poor Irishmen. They'll quarrel with anybody, the Irish will, and sometimes clear the room by swearing they'll "use their knives by Jasus"'. The women were just as bad, declared an Englishman in Liverpool in 1846. 'I never knew an Irish row in which women were not concerned; on these occasions they use anything that comes to hand; if there is nothing they fight with their fists; but they never fight with their fists if they can get a weapon.'

The 'Irish Row' became a shorthand term in the columns of provincial newspapers. Often the cause was simply drink and general rowdyness, sometimes attributed by contemporary amateur social anthropologists to the consequences of exchanging the wide-open spaces of field and bog for the cramped alleys and courts of the Victorian

Street life. Irish immigrants were often the poorest of the poor.

An earlier tumult in Stockport, in 1842, when the poor and unemployed raided the workhouse.

town. Money was frequently at the root of rows. Roger Swift's study of Victorian Wolverhampton describes a typical fracas of July 1848 when a subcontractor refused to pay fifty to a hundred navvies gathered in Bywater's Beershop in Stafford Street to receive their wages. The police were called in to rescue him, but their presence seems only to have made the situation worse. The encounter sparked off clashes between Irish navvies and the local police force that lasted throughout the week.

The Irish were frequent visitors to the courts, but their crimes were the crimes of the desperate, petty thefts and burglaries, and the sort of drink-fuelled violence we have seen above. The young were particularly highly represented. Henry Mayhew and W. Binney in their report on prisons, 'The Criminal Prisons of London', in 1862 – half of whose inmates were under twenty-five – recorded that 'the Irish constitute the poorest portion of our people and the children, therefore, are virtually orphans in this country, left to gambol in the streets and courts, without parental control, from their very earliest years … the consequence is that the child grows up not only unacquainted with any industrial occupation but untrained to habits of daily work'.

In general, contemporaries seem to have resisted the temptation to regard Irish criminality as a serious threat to the social order. Trials involving Irishmen and women were sometimes taken by newspapers as an occasion to mock the speech and behaviour of the immigrants. A *Times* report of 1824 of one domestic row has the plaintiff, a Mrs Bridget Tobin, changing her mind and pleading with the judge for clemency for her lodger. 'Mickey Mulvaney has lodged with me these seven years and a better *nathured crathur* never broke bread. I always called him a jewel of a lad. (Didn't I Mickey? – In troth you did, Biddy.)' By Biddy's account, she and Mickey were interrupted having a drink and a chat by her son, to the annoyance of Mickey, who 'took up the shovel and swore he'd split the boy's skull; so I accidentally put out my arm to save the child, and got the blow. But good-hearted soul! He never meant to hurt a hair of my head, he only meant to have split the boy's skull …'

There they are again, then, the familiar stereotypes, presented for the entertainment of *The Times*'s readers: simple, good-natured Biddy, stupid, violent, drunken Mickey. The picture drips with contempt. The couple are presented as subhuman, especially Biddy with her lack of concern for the safety of her little boy. This assessment of the Irish, though, does not present them as dangerous. They are grotesques, whose mad behaviour is a source of amusement, in much the same way as were the antics of the inmates of Bedlam.

From time to time, though, certain Irish characteristics and attitudes posed a threat to the established order. Religion was a source of conflict in Britain during the late eighteenth and nineteenth centuries, and the question of Catholic emancipation and the political status of Ireland were constants on the political agenda. Inevitably the Irish found themselves caught up in the debate, sometimes as the targets of anti-Catholic prejudice.

The Stockport Riots of June 1852 were a product of the last great upsurge of anti-papist feeling in Britain, which had waxed and waned since the Reformation, part of a pattern of clashes between English and Irish that also rocked Oldham in 1861 and London in 1862. The causes of the violence are hard to disentangle but, in the case of Stockport, religion certainly played a part. The British had by and large submitted to the new state religion with little general dissent. Catholicism was the religion of France and Spain, Britain's long-standing enemies, and adherence to Rome was a cause for suspicion. The overwhelming Catholicity of the Irish immigrants was another mark of their separateness and generally discordant relationship with respectable society. The influx of post-Famine Irish exacerbated existing anti-Catholic prejudice and coincided with political tensions over Catholic emancipation, the restoration of the Catholic hierarchy in England in 1850, and the growing influence and confidence of the Church in Britain. On 15 June 1852 the Tory government of Lord Derby banned Catholics from processing through the streets carrying symbols of their religion, in what was claimed as a peace-keeping measure, designed to prevent sectarian clashes. The *Manchester Guardian* presented an alternative explanation, which was that the move was a device to pander to anti-Catholic sentiment (a general election was three weeks away).

In Stockport the proclamation was welcomed by the Protestant establishment. Copies of it were distributed in the streets and local Orangemen posted placards urging voters not to elect a 'Papist Parliament', and slogans declaring 'To Hell with the Pope' and 'Down with the Lousy Irish' appeared chalked on walls. A procession of Stockport's Roman Catholic Sunday Schools nonetheless went ahead on 27 June. The walkers eschewed ostentatious banners but the march was preceded by a bodyguard of burly Irishmen. The day ended peacefully. The following afternoon, however, a group of Protestants paraded through the streets with an effigy of a priest and in the evening large scale sectarian fighting broke out. When the disturbances were over the Irish had come off worst. Protestant mobs attacked and wrecked houses and churches. The strongly Protestant *Stockport Advertiser* reported that the Irish were 'followed into their dwellings, dragged from their hiding places and their beds, furniture and other articles thrown into the street'. The scholar Pauline Millward's account of the episode reckons that by the end '24 Irish homes had been wrecked, an Irishman was dead, 51 Irish were injured and two Catholic chapels had been ransacked, but of 113 prisoners taken, 111 were Irish and only two were English'.

The Stockport Riots were undoubtedly fanned by local political tensions but they would not have taken place if there had not been a strong, combustible supply of anti-Catholic feeling. It was tapped into by the local paper, the *Advertiser*, which played a discreditable role in provoking antagonism while promoting the Orange cause. Its anti-Catholicism translated directly into anti-Irishness. 'What is it', an editorial asked in May 1852, 'that so often disturbs the peace of the borough, increases our rates and saps the very foundation of all our charitable institutions, but popery embodied in Irish mobs, paupers and fever patients?' The Irish were certainly not slow to react to Protestant provocations. In 1867 the anti-Catholic lectures of William Murphy, a member of the Protestant Evangelical Mission and Electoral Union, were broken up by mobs of Irishmen as he progressed around the Black Country.

While religious antagonism, stoked by local political interests, was a large factor in causing the trouble, there was an economic quarrel between the Irish and English too. The willingness of the Irish to work longer hours for less money in the cotton mills undercut the local labour market and deprived Protestants of jobs. This situation was not unique to Stockport. There are numerous examples of the Irish being used as blackleg labour and being drafted in to replace workers striking for better conditions. In Scotland the Irish were taken on to break strikes in the ironworks and mines and every strike led to an increase in the number of Irish employed. By 1848 it was calculated that more than two-thirds of miners were Irish.

There was a widespread resentment, especially among agricultural labourers, of Irish harvesters who would underbid the going rate for work. The grievance was spelled out in a verse by Ebenezer Elliot in the mid-nineteenth century.

> But work grew scarce, while bread grew dear
> And wages lessened too;
> For Irish hordes were bidders here,
> Our half-paid work to do.

The 'apartness' of the Irish in Britain placed them awkwardly in the political spectrum. As classic proletarians they might be expected to play a part in the nineteenth-century working class struggle for political power and human rights. Irishmen were indeed strongly represented in the Chartist movement, providing leaders like Feargus O'Connor and Bronterre O'Brien. Nonetheless their existence on the economic margins of society, combined with submission to the leadership of a largely conservative Catholic hierarchy, must have acted as obstacles to political development and activity. Political feeling, in so far as it was expressed at all, was engaged primarily with the status of the old country. The successes of the Irish parliamentary party and

Gladstone's conversion to Home Rule were not echoed by any great upsurge in political awareness or energy among Irish immigrants. Roger Swift has written that 'the Irish remained a much constrained and limited political element; the pauper Irish often proved difficult to register as voters'.

By the end of the century the pattern was changing and, while retaining a strong interest in the affairs of what they still regarded as their home, the Irish were increasingly a part of the mainstream political culture of Britain. For a brief period, though, it seemed that their alienation from the host nation might prove to be an asset in the revolutionary campaign of the Fenians, part of which was conducted in Britain.

Captain T. J. Kelly, a veteran of the American army, and several confederates set up the Fenian headquarters in London in January 1867, armed with credentials from the State of New York to keep them safe from the attentions of the British government. Their plan was to launch a campaign of guerrilla warfare in Ireland and Britain, which in its essentials foreshadowed the later tactics of the IRA. The uprising was scheduled for February, but to provide the military wherewithal for the action there was a plan to seize a large arms and ammunition store at Chester Castle, then rush the contents to Ireland. The plot was betrayed by an informer. The guard on the castle was strengthened and the army summoned. The raid was called off, but not before a sizeable number of Fenians had gathered in the city. A familiar series of débâcles ensued, culminating in Kelly's arrest in Manchester in September with another important Fenian, Captain Deasy. Shortly after their capture, a police van carrying them to jail was ambushed by a band of thirty men and a police sergeant guarding the men was shot dead. Kelly and Deasy got clean away. The Manchester police round-up that followed eventually produced five men who were charged with having participated in the attack. Three of them were eventually hanged – 'the 'Manchester Martyrs' – even though none of them had fired the fatal shot.

By the mid-nineteenth century, Irishmen constituted the majority of miners in Britain.

The attack on the prison van at Manchester, 1867.

In December that year came another event that fixed the Fenian menace in the mind of the British authorities and public: an attempt to rescue Richard O'Sullivan Burke, the Fenian armaments organizer who had been arrested in London and was on remand in Clerkenwell Prison in London awaiting trial. A plan to blow down the wall of the jail was fatally bungled. A massive explosion demolished the wall along with a number of houses in the street and killed twelve innocent Londoners. Another thirty were badly wounded, losing limbs and eyes.

These two events, as Robert Kee recounts, 'brought home to the English public a sense of Irish danger as nothing had ever quite done before. The very remoteness of Irish problems had always made failure to deal with them seem a somehow natural and acceptable state of affairs. Now, in the crudest way, the Irish situation had landed on the Englishman's own doorstep. It was something which had to be dealt with, if not on its own merits, at least for the sake of comfort.'

The impetus these actions provided for English politicians to treat seriously the Irish political problem was accompanied by a degree of panic on the part of the guardians of law and order. The outrages had provided evidence of the political unreliability of the strangers in their midst, reinforcing suspicions about the loyalty of the Irish to the host nation. All over the country, special constables were sworn in to be on the alert for further Fenian attacks. In the City of London alone there were 5,000 specials. In Jersey, the emergency constabulary were primed to go into action on hearing three guns fired from the fort.

Despite the fairly impressive organization the Fenians had set up in England – there were an alleged 80,000 supporters or members in 1865 – there is little evidence that the movement ever got a real grip on the heart of the immigrant population or that the Irish in Britain were psychologically conditioned to act as the succouring sea in which the revolutionaries swam. The relative political apathy of the Irish in Britain – a persistent feature – is perhaps particularly surprising in view of the hostility to which they were routinely subjected. Sometimes the British seemed to despise the Irish with a strange ferocity. It was not the antagonism that was shown to the French, who despite their frog-eating and anti-libertarian ways were at the end of the day members of the same species. In many instances, the Irish seemed to be barely accepted as human. Disraeli, who might have been thought to have had some sympathy for an outcast people, declared in 1836 that 'this wild, reckless, indolent, and uncertain and superstitious race have no sympathy with the English character. Their fair ideal of human felicity is an alternation of clannish broils and coarse idolatry. Their history describes an unbroken circle of bigotry and blood.' Later *Punch* amused its readers by claiming that 'a creature manifestly between the gorilla and the negro is to be met with in some of the lowest districts of London and Liverpool … it belongs to a tribe of Irish savages … when conversing with its kind it talks a sort of gibberish. It is, moreover, a climbing animal and may sometimes be seen climbing a ladder laden with a hod of bricks.'

The stereotyped simian Irish labourer.

This was not, of course, the entire picture. Irishmen and women could be sympathetically portayed in Victorian literature, such as the character of Phineas Finn, the attractive Irish political adventurer in a number of Trollope's novels. In real life there were Irish physicians and merchants and particularly journalists, such as T. P. O'Connor, born in Athlone in 1848, who joined the *Daily Telegraph*, was London correspondent for the *New York Herald*, entered parliament and was father of the Commons for many years.

An alternative to the simian degenerate of the *Punch* portrait is provided by the Percy French poem in which the popular Victorian songwriter notes the name of Francis Farrelly in the register when he arrives at a London hotel, and wonders if it is any of the Irishmen of that name he has known over the years.

> Or were you the Francis Farrelly I met so long ago
> In the bog below Belmullet, in the county of Mayo?
> That long-legged, freckled Francis with the deep-set, wistful eyes,
> That seemed to take their colour from those ever-changing skies.
> That put his flute together as I sketched the distant scene,
> And played me 'Planxty Kelly' and the 'Wakes of Inniskeen'.

The Irish were complex figures, then, to Victorian eyes. The middle-class conformist few could be acceptable, even lovable. The Irish who stayed in Ireland could be the subject of sentimental ballads and songs. But the poor immigrant was something else, not simply a less advantaged version of his more fortunate countryman – the Irish doctor who might treat the piles of the editor of *Punch* or the Irish journalist who might contribute to his magazine – he was cut from a different cloth. In this, it could be argued, the Victorian British were only applying, although perhaps in harsher measure, the iron rules of class with which they ordered indigenous society.

One of the key factors that distinguished the Irish from their fellow proletarians was their Catholicism. Religion was a potentially hindering factor in the immigrant's search for material comfort and social advancement, insulating him or her from the host community and making ties of friendship and marriage more difficult. Against this, the Church provided an emotional and spiritual link with the old country and a haven of warmth and friendship in what often must have seemed an ocean of cold hostility.

Catholic relief laws, which repealed discriminatory legislation, had created a climate in which the Catholic faith could be practised openly once again. However, centuries of repression had shrunk the British Catholic community and conditioned it to act with a discretion that bordered on timidity. The advent of the noisy, boisterous, unreliable Catholic Irish was far from welcome to their co-religionists, some of whom feared that the social and religious tolerance they had won by their good behaviour might be compromised by the disloyal manner and criminal antics of the newcomers. A telling exchange was recorded at a dinner party given by the Marquess of Westminster at which a number of disparaging remarks were made about Catholics. At one point the marquess referred to one of the guests, placatingly as a 'Roman Catholic Lady', to which she briskly replied, 'Yes, but an English Catholic not an Irish one, which is all the difference in the world. English Catholics are responsible beings who are taught right from wrong, whereas Irish Catholics, belonging to a yet savage nation, know no better and are perhaps excusable on that account.'

The ritual and aesthetic of Catholicism brought comfort to the urban poor.

The Catholic authorities, however, saw things differently. A strong, military cast of mind has been an abiding characteristic of the Church. If Britain was ever to be won back to Rome it needed troops. The Irish were there to provide them. As late as 1955 Cardinal Griffin was to hark back in his pastoral letter to the arrival of the Irish and to state that, but for their appearance in such numbers in the middle of the nineteenth century, the restoration of the hierarchy 'would hardly have been a possibility'. The poor Irish provided the Church with the means to expand and consolidate, to re-establish Catholicism as a popular religion rather than an upper-class sect and to make the voice of the hierarchy heard in the noisy social and economic debates of the time.

The key figure in the period was Cardinal Manning, an Englishman of the establishment without a drop of Irish blood in his veins who nonetheless identified himself strongly with the poor newcomers. His father was a member of parliament and he was educated at Harrow and Balliol before becoming an Anglican clergyman and archdeacon of Chichester. He converted to Catholicism in 1851, and by 1865 he was Archbishop of Westminster. Manning provided a bridge between the Catholic grandees of the old aristocracy in whose circles he moved comfortably and the Irish of the slums. A contemporary described him as 'more Hibernian than the Hibernians themselves in his sympathies with Ireland. A man of social position, of old family, of the highest education, and the most refined instincts, he would leave the Catholic noblemen at any time to go down to his Irish teetotallers at the East End of London.'

Manning's sympathy for the Irish nationalist movement was combined with a strong belief in the need to incorporate the labouring Irish into the social fabric of Britain, thereby guaranteeing their loyalty to its sovereign and institutions. To a certain extent this could be achieved through education, charitable institutions and self-help organizations which, as the century wore on, helped to raise the Irish from the mire at the bottom-most level of society, but much of the work of these bodies was not to come to fruition until later. Indeed it has been argued that the Church reinforced Irish Catholic segregation from Protestant-dominated society and from fuller participation in the Protestant-owned economy. A large part of the Church's function seems to have been to give spiritual solace and provide comfort and meaning in lives where material aspirations were frankly hopeless.

The judgement of Roger Swift on the condition of the pauper Irish in Britain in the middle to late nineteenth century could hardly be more bleak. They look, he writes,

> like the outcasts of Victorian society. Outcast from British capitalism as the poorest of the poor, from mainstream British politics as separatist nationalists and republicans, from the Anglo-Saxon race as 'Celts', and as Catholics from the dominant forms of British Protestantism, the Irish were the outcasts of Victorian Britain on the basis of class, nationality, race and religion, with an accumulated body of disadvantages possessed by no other group of similar size until the Eastern European, largely Jewish immigration of the late Victorian period.

Henry Edward Manning.

· 10 ·

THE FARTHEST
SHORES

O F THE MAJOR DESTINATIONS of the emigrant Irish, Australia and New Zealand were the least popular, at least if measured numerically. Yet, despite the relative paucity of numbers, the Irish constituted a much more significant proportion of the immigrant population of the Antipodes than they did in America, where at the height of emigration they constituted 10 per cent of the arriving newcomers. In Britain, as we have seen, the percentage was smaller still.

But in Australia the Irish made up 20–30 per cent of those who arrived there from the beginning of white settlement, and this figure was to remain constant for most of the nineteenth century and even into the twentieth. This fact was to ensure that in Australia the Catholic Irish had a signifi-

cantly different experience from what they had in other receiving societies. As the historian Oliver MacDonagh observes, 'The Irish were a founding people in Australia, and maintained their position in society, more or less, for almost a century and a half.' That position was likely to be at the lower end of the class scale. But the special circumstances of Australia determined that the Irish fared better there than they did elsewhere and that on the whole the experience of settlement and exile there can be said to have been a considerably happier one than it was for emigrants to America and Britain.

That it should have been so is, on the face of it, surprising. Australia was a very long way away. The voyage took up to four times as long as did the passage to America. Whereas British emigrants could console themselves with the thought that their migration was perhaps just temporary, only the most optimistic or self-deluding traveller to Australia could cling to the same comforting thought.

(*Left*) Australia was an exciting, untamed new land to Irish emigrants.
(*Above*) A family wait for the Melbourne ship in the 1870s.

Female convicts made up a substantial part of prisoners deported to the penal colony of New South Wales.

The Irish émigrés arriving after colonization of Australia began in earnest at the end of the eighteenth century included Scots Irish, attracted by the promise of a new land. But many were there involuntarily, convicts transported to the new penal settlement of New South Wales, founded in 1788 by the British as a place of banishment following the loss of the American colonies. The first to arrive came from British jails and prison hulks but there were Irish among them — in large enough numbers to merit a Fr Thomas Walshe unsuccessfully volunteering his services as Catholic chaplain. Transportation directly from Ireland began in 1791. By 1800 it is estimated that 900 of the white population of 4,500 were Irish. Of those, half were convicts and the rest were soldiers, Marines and their families. More than a quarter of the convicts seem to have been women. The failure of the 1798 uprising in Ireland brought political prisoners. The first group of seventy-one arrived in January 1800 aboard the *Minerva*.

Most of the convicts, though, were simple criminals, sent into exile for offences that would today warrant little more than a rebuke. The historian Portia Robinson records the case of thirteen-year-old Patrick Corrigan, who was playing marbles with four other boys on the steps of Parliament House in Dublin. During a friendly scuffle, one of them claimed to have been robbed. Despite a plea to the Lord Lieutenant by his respectable parents, young Patrick was convicted and sentenced with the others to be sent off to Botany Bay. The decision to transport rather than to hang or imprison seems to have been haphazard. Certainly, practical considerations appear to have loomed larger than humanitarian ones. Authority was troubled by the overcrowding in existing prisons but unwilling to spend money to build new ones. The classic picture of the hungry man, packed off in a prison ship to the wilds of Botany Bay for the crime of stealing a sheep may be a cliché, but it is not a lie.

The image of the Irish felon is etched in the history of Australia, and the activities of mythologized criminal rebels like Jack Donohue and Ned Kelly have given rise to the notion that the Irish were a particularly intractable and difficult element in white Australian society. But as Donald Harman Akenson points out, the Irish were not a disproportionate element of the convict population. They comprised roughly 25 per cent of the criminals sent to the penal colonies at a time when the Irish share of the United Kingdom's population was roughly 30 per cent. The political element was small. Between 1788 and 1853, when transportation to the eastern Australian colonies was abandoned, fewer than 1.5 per cent of Irish convicts had been found guilty of political crimes.

During that time, 48,000 Irish criminals, men and women, were sent from Ireland and Britain to Australia. Arriving alongside them were an ever growing number of voluntary settlers, and the two communities mingled. With time the convict element declined. Professor Akenson estimates that 'well before the middle of the nineteenth century most of the Irish-born population of the Australian colonies was composed of free immigrants, not convicts or former convicts'.

During the Famine years some 15,000 Irish migrants arrived in Victoria — a substantial number but nothing like the numbers flooding into North America and Britain. The real surge came with the discovery of gold in Ballarat in Victoria in August 1851. Mostly lured by the gold, some 84,000 Irish arrived in the Australian colonies during the 1850s, and the majority stayed on to settle.

Gold diggers at a forest creek, Mount Alexander, Port Phillip.

Even with the prospect of striking it rich, the thought of travelling to the opposite end of the earth was a daunting one. Australia was more mysterious than America, which popular literature and émigré letters had made familiar at even the remotest firesides of rural Ireland. A decisive factor in drawing the Irish there – and one which did not apply to America or Britain – was the existence of assisted passages. The first governmental schemes to pay the costs of migrants to New South Wales and Van Diemen's Land (Tasmania) began in 1831 and later the main colonies developed their own projects. The Irish were particularly quick to exploit the opportunities. Although they were only 30 per cent of the population of the British Isles, they made up 52 per cent of the assisted migrants to New South Wales and what was to become Victoria in the years 1837–50. The religious affiliations of Irish migrants to Australia in general equated to those of Ireland itself. In 1911, of Irish-born persons living in Australia, 71.3 per cent were Catholic, 14.1 per cent Anglican, 8.7 per cent Presbyterian and the rest members of other Protestant sects. Even though many of the Protestants hailed from Ulster counties they came from the Anglo-Irish rather than Ulster Scots parts of it, namely Tyrone, Fermanagh and Armagh.

The assisted passage schemes were supplemented by initiatives by the British government. In response to demand from Australian employers, some 4,000 young girls and women orphaned in the Famine were transported to the colonies to work as domestic servants. The experience must have been an often frightening one, full of uncertainty and the disorientation of dislocation. Arriving in Sydney the women were taken to what had been a convict barracks where prospective employers would come and vet them. Their fortunes varied. Only a third of them, for whatever reason, married Irishmen. Some of them had happy and fulfilling lives. Fate brought others full circle, and some women ended up in the same sort of charitable institutions from which they had set out.

Irish drovers with a Jesuit priest,
Fr Browne, near Gobabla.

The lives of the orphan girls reflect a characteristic we see in many of the Irish settlers in Australia: a determination to throw themselves into the new society and to make the best of things. Perhaps the very distance from the old country — which with the heat and exotic flora and fauna of Australia must have seemed to have a planetary remoteness — precluded the melancholy yearnings for the homeland that were expressed in the songs and poetry of American and even British exiles from Ireland. Similarly, the bitterness towards the British that marked the political thought of the Irish Americans seems to have been less pronounced in the psyche of the Irish Australians.

The fact that for many emigrants passage was free does not mean that they were in the lowest stratum of economic exiles. In general, it seems that the sort of people who made the trip to Australia were slightly higher up the social scale than their counterparts boarding vessels to Liverpool or New York. Oliver MacDonagh notes that 'state assistance, with its stress upon certified respectability and stable employment, tended generally to favour what we might call the petit bourgeoisie, or upper working class, rather than the proletariat of the Irish countryside …' I estimate that the great majority were drawn from say, the third, fourth and fifth rather than the sixth and seventh rankings in the scale.'

Voyages might have been much longer than the Atlantic crossing but they were well organized and more comfortable. The diary of a young Protestant lady, Minnie Williams, who left Ireland for New Zealand in 1881 with her parents, three sisters and brother in the *Zealandia*, an iron clipper, records a typical experience of the assisted migrant. The food is good and plentiful (though later it runs short), with a

The Australian landscape was wild and exotic after Ireland.

bottle of lime juice a week for everyone in the tropical part of the passage. The changing scene is noted with awe ('I never saw a more beautiful sky and sunset in my life') but the excitement of anticipation is eventually punctured by the fact of arrival ('Friday, 30th September. Alongside the wharf, can go on shore when we like . . . Kate, Emma and I are disgusted with the place, would give anything to be back again. All the rest are delighted').

The Williams family were a typical example of chain migrants, moving along a well-tested governmentally supervised route about which they were given plenty of information. Minnie's brother Sam was already in place to welcome them. Such an experience was far from unusual. The smooth running of the machine meant that new arrivals were less likely to pile up at the first landfall, as was so often the case in the United States and Britain, where many migrants never made it beyond New York or Liverpool.

In fact, the Irish were geographically distributed with remarkable evenness in Australia. Heavy Celtic concentrations in specific corners of the country were a feature of Irish immigration to both America and Britain. In Britain they headed for Lancashire, Clydeside and London, in America for the great cities of the eastern seaboard and the mill towns and manufacturing centres of the interior. Whole quarters, in America whole towns, became predominantly Irish. In Australia, though, the Irish were spread substantially through every part of the land. As we have seen, the Australian element in the Irish exodus was small – 5 per cent of all those who went overseas at most. In Australian terms, however, it was huge, a little less than a quarter of those who arrived between 1788 and the end of the nineteenth century.

Typical pioneer home at Pomeroy village, New South Wales.

There were, of course, fluctuations in the density of the Irish in Austalia. In Anglophile South Australia they made up only 17–18 per cent of the population and 15 per cent in the former convict settlement of Tasmania. But MacDonagh calculates that if you divided Australia into large chunks you would find a minimum proportion of 15 per cent Irish and a maximum of 35 per cent in any given area – a remarkable consistency when compared with the pattern in America and Britain. The Irish lived where everyone else did. They settled in proportionate numbers on the land (unlike in America, where the Catholic Irish were under-represented in the rural population) and in the cities, where they avoided coagulating into ghettos. The presence of wide-open spaces was a powerful attraction to people whose economic fate had depended on access to land in a crowded island and the historian Patrick O'Farrell points out that 'from the beginning of Australian settlement the Irish exhibited a veritable obsession with the acquisition of land and livestock'.

They could not entirely avoid the fate of the poor immigrant. The jobs they got were often as bad as those obtained by their brother and sister emigrants in America and Britain. The Irish were heavily present in the ranks of unskilled labourers and domestic workers. But, unlike in Britain, this was not almost all they did. They were much more visible in middle-class and professional occupations than their counterparts in America and England. The lack of access to capital meant they were rarely merchants, bankers or brokers. But they were familiar figures in professions like medicine and the law, and in the practice of politics and journalism, even predominating in some fields. In Victoria in the latter part of the nineteenth century, the first six Speakers of the Legislative Assembly were Irish born, as were half the members of some of the state cabinets of this period and three-quarters of the attorneys and solicitors general. Some of the newcomers were already distinguished. Charles Gavan Duffy, the largely self-educated champion of northern Catholics, arrived in Melbourne with his wife and family in 1856, having declared he could no longer bear the political climate in Ireland. He started practising law but was persuaded into politics and in time became premier of Victoria. His son, Frank, was to serve as chief justice of the High Court of Australia.

In agriculture, the Irish were proportionately represented, but tended to have poorer farms. They were to be found in great numbers in some colonial police forces and in some trades such as the liquor business. MacDonagh concludes that 'generally, of course, the lower the occupation in the lower scale the higher proportion of Irish Catholics among its members'. But the social and economic obstacles facing the Irish immigrant were much less daunting than those confronting him in Britain and even in America.

The rough and tumble of colonial society seems to have been to the taste of the newcomers. The British were there of course. But they were in many cases themselves a part of the struggle, rather than a negative factor in it. The land was wild, and white complicity in the shared struggle to tame it meant racial and class differences were reduced. The relative smallness of the Famine element in the ranks of the émigrés – only 75,000 of the two million or so 'Famine emigrants' of 1846–56 headed south – meant that hatred of the British as oppressors, even the architects of genocide, was minimalized. Scholars have sometimes seen Australia as a *tabula rasa*, offering laboratory conditions in which they can observe Irish behaviour that is relatively undistorted by economic, religious and political oppression. We shall return in a later chapter to the

Sheep-shearing in the 1920s.

question of the extent to which the fate of Irish emigrants is determined by the characteristics of the society in which they find themselves. But the crude conclusion that can be drawn is that, exposed to the relatively benign economic, social and political conditions of emerging Australia, the Irish proved to be remarkably normal.

Of course there were rebels. When the government tried to impose a licence fee on the prospectors digging in the goldfields of Victoria it was an Irishman, Peter Lalor, who led the resistance. A pitched battle between 150 miners who refused to pay the fee and nearly 300 policemen at Bakery Hill just outside the township of Eureka ended with some thirty men being killed, five of whom were colonial troops. There were more Irish among the dead than any other nationality, and the encounter is remembered as a key event in the history of the Australian labour movement.

The stories of Irish rebels like Jack Donahue and Ned Kelly reveal the tenacity of a tradition of rural violence imported by some of the newcomers. Donahue was transported from Dublin in 1825, arrived in NSW, escaped and set off with a band of accomplices to prey on settlers in the Bathurst area for two years before being shot dead by the police. He was mythologized in a mawkish ballad which chose to present him as a victim of political oppression rather than as a parasitical criminal.

> This bold undaunted highwayman as you may understand
> Was banished for his natural life from Erin's happy land.
> Dublin, city of renown, where his first breath he drew,
> 'Twas there they christened him the brave and bold Jack Donahue.

More famous still was Ned Kelly. Ned Kelly's father John was popularly supposed to have been transported from Tipperary in 1840 for stealing two pigs. Research has suggested a less clichéd picture of injustice. 'Red' Kelly may well have been a more serious robber who, when caught, reduced his sentence by giving evidence to the police. After serving time in Tasmania in 1848 he crossed to the mainland and took up residence near Melbourne. In 1850 he married Ellen Quinn, being forced to elope with her in the face of fierce resistance from her father John, who was opposed to his daughter marrying a convict. He moved away from Melbourne, in an apparent attempt to stay out of trouble. It did not work. In 1865 he was charged with cattle stealing and died the following year. The Quinn–Kelly clan were a nightmare collection of criminals and drunkards who lived in a perpetual state of feuding and conflict with the law. Ellen Kelly was a classic outlaw matriarch who sold grog to make ends meet and at the age of forty-two remarried a Californian man half her age who was a renowned horse thief. She indoctrinated her sons to believe that no Irishman could expect justice in an English court and that the police were lackeys of English landlords. Ned Kelly seems to have learned these lessons well. The two documents he left behind to justify his actions and expound his primitive political philosophy, the 'Cameron' and 'Jerilderie' letters, are full of anti-English invective and hatred of the police.

Ned was first in trouble with the police in 1871 for violent assault. Shortly after getting out of prison he was charged with stealing a horse. He has been deemed unlucky in this matter – there was genuine confusion about the horse's ownership. In any case, he was sentenced to three years and on his release took on the man he

Ned Kelly photographed at Melbourne Jail the day before he was hanged on 11 November 1880.

The Kelly gang's last stand at Glenrowan.

Kelly's crude iron armour.

blamed for his misfortunes in a twenty-round bare-knuckle fight. Prison had sobered him nonetheless. He took a job in the lumber business and seems to have prospered reasonably for a while. In 1877 he ended up in court after a drunken spree. Some time the same year a powerful rancher in the corner of north east Victoria where Kelly was living blamed him for the disappearance of some of his stock and warrants were issued for his arrest and that of his brother Dan. When a policeman called Fitzpatrick tried to apprehend them he was shot in the wrist. The boys' mother Ellen, who had recently given birth, was arrested as an accomplice and sentenced to three years in prison.

The boys, together with two other young men of Irish stock, took to the Wombat hills. They clashed with a police patrol and killed three of the officers. The police launched a big operation to capture them, alienating local opinion by holding for long periods people aiding the outlaws and in the process building sympathy for the Kelly gang. With nothing to lose the Kellys turned to bank robbery, pulling off two daring raids at Eoroa and Jerilderie. The price on their heads mounted. So too did Ned Kelly's ambitions. In June 1880 he and the gang planned to take over the village of Glenrowan. A schoolmaster whom Ned Kelly had spared tipped off the police and the gang was surrounded. Ned had a chance to escape but, when it became clear that his companions were doomed, returned to fight it out with the police. The academic James Sturgis records him looming 'out of the morning mist,' seemingly larger than life, encased in home-made iron armour'. The rest of the gang were killed. Kelly was brought down by bullets aimed at his legs and put on trial. On being sentenced to death he told the judge, 'I will see you where I go.' The superstitious were awestruck when the judge died ten days later.

There is much that is attractive in the figure of Ned Kelly, with his quick — albeit knockabout — wit, bravery and loyalty to his family and comrades. He saw himself as something more than a lovable villain, however. In the 'Jerilderie' letter of 1879 he declares that 'a policeman is a disgrace to his country … in the first place he is a rogue in his heart, but too cowardly to follow it up without having the force to disguise it. Next he is a traitor to his country, ancestors and religion.' Kelly did not have to specify that the policemen in question were Irish policemen. As historian Edith Mary Johnston has pointed out, the patrol that first clashed with the Kellys in the Wombat hills were all Irish. At their head was Sergeant Michael Kennedy, married with five children, an officer of excellent reputation who arrived in Victoria in 1859 from County Westmeath. Kelly wounded then killed him. His ear was later cut off, which was a traditional mutilation carried out by the Whiteboy terrorists of rural Ireland. Constables Lonigan and Scanlon, also shot dead, were both first-generation immigrants. The fourth, Constable Thomas Newman McIntyre, was an Orangeman, originally from Belfast. His survival was probably due to luck, but there has been speculation that Kelly regarded Protestant policemen as less deserving of his wrath than the Catholics.

Many of the innumerable cases that brought the Kelly–Quinn clan before the law were heard by Irish magistrates and judges, many of whom were products of Trinity College Dublin and former members of the Protestant Ascendancy. The judge who sentenced Kelly to death, Sir Redmond Barry, was also a Protestant, born in County Cork. Sir Redmond's life and career shows up the archaism of Kelly's histrionics. He had been sympathetic to the Eureka diggers and acquitted them of treason. Throughout the 1840s he regularly acted, unpaid, as defence counsel for aborigines charged with serious offences against white settlers. Among his friends were George Higginbotham from Dublin, who arrived in Melbourne in 1854. Higginbotham became editor of the *Argus* newspaper where he expounded radical views, before going into law and ending up chief justice of Victoria.

George Higginbotham: kind to children and drunks.

He has been described by Professor Manning Clark, in his classic history of Australia, as 'a man with Christ-like qualities who spent much of his time with lawyers and accountants, a gentle spirit who found himself with the measurers, an enlarger surrounded by straiteners … He was kind to drunks, whom he sheltered from the self-righteous, tender with women and very gentle with little children.' During the maritime strike of 1891 he openly sent £50 plus a further £10 a week for the relief of the strikers' families. He was elected attorney general on a platform of 'manhood suffrage, total separation of church from state, state aid to denominational education, reform of land tenures and an abhorrence of faction and cabal'.

These were Irishmen of the establishment, then, vigorously espousing policies and causes that any working Irishman or woman could agree with. They were in Australia not to perpetuate the misrule of the Ascendancy but to forge a new country in which the mistakes and abuses of the system they had left behind would not be repeated.

Despite the balladeering and myth-making that Kelly's brief and violent life generated, it is hard to believe that his rebel posturings were taken seriously by many outside his immediate circle. His words and actions mirror those of the rural societies of the old country with their implicit belief in the injustice of landlords and the threat and use of terror to assert power over them. But the situation in Australia was very different. Irish immigrants had, potentially, as much to lose from lawlessness as other Australians. Kelly was undoubtedly a product of the Irish tradition of primitive rebellion. But he cannot be said to have been representative of any widespread feeling among the people he sprang from. Nonetheless, there are themes of egalitarianism in his conduct, respect for and solidarity with one's mates, that would find favour with successive generations of Australian men, and not just those of Irish origin.

Far from being revolutionaries, the Irish in general swam in the mainstream of the political development of the country. They were found everywhere. In the great majority of parliamentary constituencies, particularly those of the relatively populous eastern crescent of Australia, they made up one-sixth to one-quarter of the electorate. In such proportions the Irish were unable to assert themselves as a discrete, decisive force. MacDonagh notes that 'completely independent political action by the Catholic Irish community was generally doomed to failure, and certain to fail if it produced a hostile coalescence of the other groups and interests. Conversely, it might be powerful if combined with one or more of the larger exogenous elements.'

Thus, the Catholic Irish lobby could play a key role in crucial issues of nineteenth- and early-twentieth-century Australian history, involving itself, often radically, in questions of land distribution and labour rights, secular and denominational education and constitutional matters, including relations with Britain. The Irish have been presented as a dynamic yet constructive force in Australian politics, a sort of 'loyal opposition'. One voice that seems to exemplify this attitude is that of Daniel Deniehy, the son of a convict and another journalist-cum-lawyer. Born in 1828, he was taken on a tour of England, Ireland and other countries in Europe as an adolescent and was greatly impressed by Daniel O'Connell, one of whose monster rallies he attended. During the debate on the shape of the constitution of New South Wales he ranged himself against the landowners and conservatives attempting to reproduce British political models in the new land, notably an upper chamber based on the House of Lords whose membership would be determined by right of birth. The newspaper account of the day reports him pouring scorn on the 'Botany Bay aristocrats'. The *Herald* wrote that he was 'puzzled how to classify them. They could not aspire to the miserable and effete dignity of the grandees of Spain. They had antiquity of birth, but these he would defy any naturalist properly to classify . . . perhaps it was only a specimen of the remarkable contrariety that existed in the Antipodes. Here, they all knew, the common water mole was transformed into the duck-billed platypus. And in some distant emulation of this degeneration, he supposed they were to be favoured with a bunyip aristocracy.' This witty and deadly invective can be seen as belonging to a tradition of robust Australian political discourse that lives on today in the rhetoric of such masters of the genre as the former prime minister Paul Keating, himself of Irish descent.

It has been pointed out that the type of Irish politics practised in America, where weight of numbers could secure power and control, albeit in a localized and sectionalized fashion, was impractical in Australia. Conversely, the power Irish Australians did wield was spread wide in the land. And whatever the restrictions on their room to manoeuvre, they were far more effective than their brethren in Britain, whose electoral power was puny.

The mild temper of Irish Australians is well illustrated by their preferences in Irish politics. There were Fenian associations in the 1860s, the years of the Brotherhood's ascent, but the revolutionary message failed to gain adherents in any serious numbers. The Home Rule movement led by Charles Stuart Parnell, on the other hand, had many supporters and was very well organized in Irish Australia, and succeeded in raising impressive amounts of money for the cause. MacDonagh's explanation is that Home Rule equated to the sort of colonial autonomy that Australia was in the process of securing for itself. It seemed a realizable, practical political goal which fitted the mood of the host society. Furthermore it must also have chimed with the aspirational nature of the Australian immigrants themselves, many of whom were eager to get on and anxious not to antagonize a nation in which the connection with Britain did not chafe in the same way that it had in America. Finally, economic conditions were not so onerous that they were likely to produce a resentment that might lead to extremes. Pay may have been poor in the colonies and job security uncertain. But Irish immigrants, by and large, did not face the alienating exploitation and poverty of their counterparts in the docks of Liverpool or the mills of New England. There was always hope, and the paths to prosperity and respectability were much wider and less strewn with obstacles than elsewhere. A census survey of 1933 which correlates religion to income showed that Catholics (which at this time meant, largely, the Irish) were distinctly but undramatically under-represented in the two top income categories and over-represented to a minor degree in the lowest. In the middle they did not vary much from national averages. This picture may look unremarkable enough but it represented a median status among the Irish in Australia that was unlikely to provoke any outré political thinking.

As Donald Harman Akenson concludes,

> what really stands out about the Irish migrants to Australia is seemingly a contradiction in terms: once the convict period was over, the Irish migrants were distinguished by their very ordinariness. They were good solid representatives of Irish migrants throughout the diaspora: neither overly skilled nor overly proletarian, balanced in their gender ratio, and representative of the Protestant-Catholic proportions of the homeland. Good Irish people.

The same can be said of the migrants to New Zealand. They too were a fairly typical slice of Irish emigrants generally, young, both men and women in equal numbers, mostly unskilled but with a sprinkling of skilled and middle class, the majority of them Catholic. Enthusiastic reports in the Irish press and from letters home spread the word that New Zealand was an attractive spot especially for the land hungry, with a better climate and better soil than Australia. The islands had become a British possession after the Maori population ceded sovereignty in 1840 in exchange for protection and guaranteed possession of lands (a promise which was soon broken). The government of New Zealand was not initially well disposed towards Irish immigration, preferring to attract settlers of English stock. A low level of antipathy existed, particularly towards Catholics. The pressing need for men, and particularly women, to settle the land and provide labour forced the government to overcome its prejudice. The Irish tide swept in. Further waves followed, after the government allowed settlers to nominate family and friends for assisted passages, a system which the Irish were particularly adept at exploiting to set up busy lines of chain migration.

By the end of the nineteenth century the Irish made up 18.7 per cent of the non-Maori population. Of these, the great majority were Catholics. As late as 1951 they made up 16.7 per cent. On arrival they spread themselves around the country, settling in the same proportions in town and country as the rest of the population. The absence of ghettos seems a sure indication that the Irish were at home in the new land and felt no need to huddle together for protection or emotional and spiritual warmth.

The picture of fitting in easily is borne out by a survey of the New Zealand census authorities in 1921 which showed that male Irish Catholics were in the same jobs in the same proportions as everyone else. The most common occupation for Irishmen was farming, just as it was for the rest of the male population. These figures are important for, as Akenson points out, they show that there was nothing in the cultural background of Catholic migrants from Ireland to New Zealand that prevented them and their children from doing as well as anyone else. Often they were coming from a rural background with an understanding of farm life that was a good preparation for agricultural frontier life. Beyond that, the experience of New Zealand seems proof of something else. That is, that there was nothing in the inherent nature of Irishness or Catholicity that could be regarded as an obstacle to success and achievement in a new society. The lesson of Australia and New Zealand was that, given a reasonable opportunity and the absence of severe general or institutional hostility, the Irish could be sewn in almost seamlessly alongside their fellow countrymen and achieve a normality that rendered their ethnicity little more than an identifying badge to be displayed according to desire.

The experience of the Irish in the culturally familiar environments of Australia and New Zealand contrasts strongly with the story of Irish immigration to Argentina. Descendants of the Wild Geese who ended up in Spain were well represented among the administrative elite who colonized Spanish America. After Argentina rebelled against Spain in 1810, manpower shortages and the prominent presence of Irishmen in the military and merchant class opened up a flow of immigrants from Ireland to Argentina. The historian Patrick McKenna's work on the subject has established that when emigrants began arriving in considerable numbers in the mid-1820s they were mostly the younger, non-inheriting sons, and later daughters, of larger tenant farmers and leaseholders. They sailed from Liverpool to Buenos Aires, a voyage that took three months and cost the not inconsiderable sum of £16. Many seem to have had their tickets pre-paid by family or friends *in situ* or by employers.

Most spent time in Buenos Aires working in Irish-owned meat-curing factories, learning the language and saving money before moving out to herd sheep in the

A street in Buenos Aires in the late nineteenth century. The Irish immigrant experience in Argentina was characterized by their struggle to retain a separate identity. Eventually, the community was pulled towards increased assimilation.

lands which became available as the Argentinian army cleared them of their Indian populations. Shepherds worked on a share basis, in which the owner would supply the immigrant with a flock which he would tend for an agreed number of years. At the end of the contract the expanded flock was divided and profits on wool clippings shared. Life on the pampas was lonely and hard for the shepherds. 'Many never returned,' recounts McKenna, 'or returned broken in body and spirit, sometimes insane from years of almost complete solitude. A broken leg or a fall from a horse frequently meant a lingering death from thirst or starvation.' Those who made it, though, were set up and well placed to take advantage of the opportunities opened up by the big land sales and the growth of the cattle industry in the 1850s.

The senior figures in the Irish community in Argentina worked hard to keep the immigrant community together, at least partly in order to form a united economic front. Inevitably, the Catholic Church provided the necessary cohesion. The dominant figure was Fr Anthony Fahy, a brewer's son from Loughrea in Galway, who arrived to be chaplain to the Irish emigrants in 1843. He made it his work to ensure that, as far as was possible, the Irish were insulated from the local population. The newcomers were met off the boat and placed in approved, Irish-run boarding houses. The young men were found jobs in the meat-curing houses or on *estancias*. The young women were encouraged to choose a husband swiftly from among the shepherds and landowners passing through town on business, at specially arranged dances.

Fr Fahy joined forces with the leading Irish merchant, Thomas Armstrong, a Protestant from Athlone, who became banker to the Irish community. He managed the financial affairs of his flock, and established charitable foundations to run schools – the Fahy Institute and Clonmacnoise for boys and St Brigid's for girls – and to import priests and nuns from Ireland. The Irish community thrived. But they did so in semi-isolation. Fr Fahy's great organizational energy was bent to minimizing the risk of assimilation. It was, ultimately, a hopeless task. After General Juan Perón came to power in 1946, schools were forced to abandon ethnicity as a criterion for admission and they closed or lost their Irish character. Economic changes meant the Irish began to drift to the cities to work. The pace of assimilation accelerated, and today the process is almost complete.

The story of the Irish in Argentina is an anomalous one. It shows that even in a non-Anglophone country they could survive and prosper, using their separateness as a tool to advance the community. In the end, though, their numbers were too small (perhaps 30,000 Irishmen and women emigrated) to maintain their ethnic and cultural distance from their hosts.

The path of separateness was not available to the Irish in the two great centres of emigration. In the emergent American nation and the well-established society of Britain, the great ambition was to fit in. Survival remained a struggle for many. To prosper still required a high degree of extraordinariness. But, as the new century opened and the great population movements slowed down, the story of Irish emigration in both places was entering a new phase.

· II ·

TWENTIETH-CENTURY IDENTITY

AS THE TWENTIETH CENTURY progressed, the Irish finally graduated to statehood. At the same time as Ireland came of age as an independent nation with the creation of the Free State in 1921, Irish people abroad were being fully accepted into the ranks of the nations to which they had emigrated. The stigma of being Irish faded as new waves of immigrants took their place in the bottom stratum of society. In America, the Irish not only survived and prospered; in many cases they triumphed. The apotheosis was reached with the election as president in 1960 of John Fitzgerald Kennedy, a man whose Irishness was not merely acknowledged but vaunted. In Britain, the process of integration was much more unobtrusive. Frequently the descendants of the starveling inhabitants of the rookeries and slums adopted the protective colouring of the surrounding environment and were absorbed into the host society. It is worth remembering that Britain too had an 'Irish' premier in the shape of James Callaghan. Little or nothing, though, was made of his ethnic origins.

In the twentieth century Irish Americans came into their own, economically, politically, socially and culturally. Could the same be true of their British counterparts? The question is difficult to answer due to the very different social circumstances that prevailed in the two main centres of the expatriate Irish and their descendants. In America, many of the Irish immigrants lost any sense of ethnic or religious separateness and gratefully lowered themselves into the melting pot, marrying out of race or creed, and converting to Protestantism. There nonetheless remained a large, identifiable bulk of Irish Americans whose progress can be charted, proud of their origins but unshakeably loyal to the United States and its values.

(*Left*) Irish American Dodgers fans celebrating victory in the Brooklyn Tavern, New York.
(*Above*) Fitting in. A veteran of the Royal Irish Rifles serves a peacetime pint in a London pub.

The British Irish are a much better-camouflaged group. The processes of inter-marriage and assimilation, and a cultural and political climate that made it undesirable and probably pointless to advertise ethnicity, have rendered them harder to spot on the broad canvas of twentieth-century Britain.

The great movements of the Irish out of their homeland slowed down in the new century. Emigration was still a fact of life, a choice that faced every young man and woman as they approached adulthood. But the wholesale denuding of the island's youth that had occurred in the Famine years and the 1860s and 1880s was at an end. In the first two decades of the century, the outflow plummeted. At the same time the choice of destination switched. More people went to Britain now than to America. This was partly due to a change of attitudes towards immigration in America. The country was filling up and a quota system was established. The emergency legislation designed to handle the influx of Europeans fleeing from the devastation of the First World War gave Great Britain and Ireland an allocation of 77,342. In 1924 this was superseded by a measure which recognized the Free State and set the quota for its citizens at 28,567. Five years later it was reduced to 17,853.

By now, the Irish in America were no longer an immigrant community as such, but part of the warp and weft of a dynamic society. According to Professor Akenson's calculation, 'from the 1920s onward Irish Catholics in the USA were above average socio-economically, and by the 1960s they were a privileged group'. It will be noted that we are talking about Irish *Catholics* here. As their fortunes waxed, those of the Protestants declined. According to a comparative study by Andrew Greeley, the Catholics climbed above the line into the ranks of the privileged in the decade of the First World War. Irish Protestants slid below it probably during the 1930s.

One possible, tentative explanation for this dramatic split in fortunes is provided by geography. By the middle of the century 70 per cent of Catholics had gravitated to the north east and north central United States, where they led overwhelmingly urban lives. Half of the Protestants lived in the South. Most of them were also city-dwellers, but 30 per cent of the population was rural.

The Irish Catholics proved skilful in adapting to and exploiting the big city environment. In 1963 Senator Daniel Patrick Moynihan wrote, 'New York used to be an Irish city. Or so it seemed. There were sixty or seventy years when the Irish were everywhere.' The Irish hegemony lasted until well after the Second World War. A classic figure was the Irish-born William O'Dwyer, mayor from 1945 to 1950, an ex-policeman who had entered politics. The police and fire departments were heavily Irish, as were many teachers and other city workers. Most religious New Yorkers were Catholics and the Church hierarchy was dominated by Irish priests, headed by Francis, Cardinal Spellman, the son of Irish parents, who continued the tradition of political muscle-flexing established by predecessors such as Archbishop Hughes. Like Hughes he was conservative, often controversially so. He supported the anti-communist campaigns of Senator Joe McCarthy in the 1940s and 1950s. On spiritual matters he was a critic of the modernizing reforms

Three children chat to their local priest, Father Kelly, on the steps of the church in Harlem, New York, 1955. The Church spread Irish influence throughout American society.

of the theological conference body, Vatican II. And he earned the admiration of President Lyndon Johnson and the disapproval of Church liberals for the backing he gave to America's prosecution of the Vietnam War.

Spellman's hard-line positions did not necessarily put him out of step with Irish New York opinion. There was a deep strain of social conservatism in the city's Catholics. McCarthy was a hero to the New York Police Department. As the immigrants and their descendants moved up the social scale their attitudes, inevitably, grew more conservative. From the end of the Second World War prosperity drew the Irish out of the city to the growing housing estates of Long Island, New Jersey and Westchester, so that by 1950 more than half the metropolitan area's Irish Americans lived outside the city. In their place came blacks and Hispanics. The Democratic party was no longer the natural home of the Irish. In the 1964 presidential election some 55 per cent of New York Irish voters cast their ballots for the ultra-conservative Barry Goldwater.

In the right candidate, though, Irishness could always attract Irish voters. And there was never a candidate who played the card more adeptly than John Fitzgerald Kennedy. Kennedy could be seen as a sort of secular patron saint of the Irish nation, second only to St Patrick. But in particular he was an object of veneration to Irish immigrants. His family story encapsulated the epic elements of the immigrants' experience, reproducing many of the details of their own lives. His personality, at least as publicly presented, reflected the best Irish immigrant qualities of bravery, determination, dash and humanity. The Kennedy saga is now so clouded with myth and fantasy that it is difficult to discern any more the great ordinariness of the dynasty's origins. One of the strongest elements in his appeal to the Irish at home and abroad was that his political and social apotheosis raised their own standing. An Irishman, three generations away from the bottom of the social pile, had made it to the most powerful position in the free world.

The Magnificent Kennedys.

'Honey Fitz' and grandson, John F. Kennedy, pictured 1945–6.

JFK's maternal and paternal ancestors were both Famine refugees. On the Fitzgerald side they had gone into the grocery and liquor businesses which traditionally attracted the entrepreneurially minded Irish. Then politics beckoned. John F. Fitzgerald was successively elected city councilman, state senator, congressman and finally mayor of Boston from 1905 to 1914. He was a thoroughly modern politician to whom his grandson owed a great deal for his style. He worked hard at establishing himself as the voice of cultural unity, constantly emphasizing the essential patriotism of the Irish and the contribution they had made in building America and would continue to make. He was a gifted phrase-maker, coining slogans that rang with energy and optimism, famously promising a 'bigger, better and busier Boston'. Above all he broke down barriers. The academic Alun Munslow has written that Fitzgerald was 'a conduit through which flowed the hegemonic cultural stream. This stream became a river that renegotiated Irishness and Catholicism in urban America, and forced open hitherto closed political doors. The most important of these doors were those of the White House.'

'Honey Fitz' in some ways embodied the positive elements in the Irish immigrant urge to prosper in the new country. He was intelligent and charming, imaginative enough to recognize his opponents' fears and devise strategies for dealing with them. In Joseph Kennedy, JFK's father, we see the immigrant's darker face. It is instructive that Joe Kennedy shoved his in-laws into the background and frequently belittled them when he encountered them. 'Who are all those freeloaders?' he yelled at an aide during a reception he had given to mark his son's inauguration, affecting not to recognize a party of Fitzgeralds helping themselves at the buffet.

Joe Kennedy lacked public-spiritedness except when it was politically expedient. His politics were neanderthal, despising the weak and the poor and worshipping power even if it was Adolf Hitler who wielded it. He was rapacious for money and sex and believed that, ultimately, everything was a matter of price. Repellent though he may have been as a human being, these traits can be regarded as being as much a logical response to the immigrant experience as the inclusiveness and humanity of his father-in-law. Joe Kennedy, one senses, felt very strongly his proximity to the gutter and saw in money the most effective way of insulating himself from it and drawing himself and his family so high above it as to render the prospect of a tumble down the social scale to the bottom of the ladder impossible. In short, Honey Fitz believed in talking his way into the heart of American political and social life. Joe Kennedy put his faith in buying his way in.

In JFK, both immigrant strategies for success were combined. From his grandfather he inherited charm, intelligence and political nous. From his father he got ruthlessness, greed and of course the wherewithal to pursue his ambitions. It was a dynamic combination. In it, his supporters and fans could see what they wanted to see. The flashing smile and twinkling eyes, the legacy of Grandfather Fitzgerald, masked the paternal amorality that made it possible.

The election of John Fitzgerald Kennedy in 1960 marked the high point in the political and social achievement of the Catholic Irish in America. There had been presidents of Irish stock before. But they had been Protestants, and their ethnicity had played little part in their political make-up. Kennedy harped on his roots, making a trip to the old country to visit the townland from where his ancestors sprang. Much of the identification with origins was cynical. He chose, after all, to marry a socialite

Going 'home'. JFK visits relatives and his ancestral townland near New Ross, County Wexford.

with no claim to Irish blood and one of the drawbacks to becoming president, he moaned to a confidant, was that he would have to put in the occasional highly-publicized appearance at Mass.

Nonetheless, Kennedy's recognition of and emphasis on his Irishness endorsed the notion that Irishness was acceptable, even desirable, and, for the moment at least, fashionable. This idea was not new. It had been some time in the making, promoted in book, film and song. Popular culture from the end of the nineteenth century had been building up in layered accretions an image of Irishness that was by and large highly complimentary and respectful. The sly and drunken Paddies and Biddies were long forgotten. In their place were handsome men and pretty women, marked by their courage, wit and general *joie de vivre*.

This sentimental picture was propagated by the Irish themselves, in the cinema by John Ford, whose films of the West contained idealized frontier Irish characters like the Sergeant in *She Wore a Yellow Ribbon* (1949), a bit of a boozer perhaps, but warmhearted, courageous and loyal. His pictures about Ireland, particularly *The Quiet Man* (1952), paint a highly sentimental and inaccurate portrait of his spiritual homeland. Actors of Irish stock peopled his movies, such as Victor McLaglen and John Wayne, whose Scots Irish great-great-grandfather had been a United Irishman in County Antrim and emigrated after the failure of the rebellion. Ford claimed to have been

John Ford's *She Wore a Yellow Ribbon*. Victor McLaglen (*far left*) is the sergeant with a fondness for the bottle.

baptized Sean Aloysius O'Feeney, the son of an immigrant from County Galway. He visited Ireland in 1921 and encountered relatives connected with the IRA whose cause he supported all his life. It was an Irish film, *The Informer* (1935), based on a novella by Liam O'Flaherty that made his reputation. But it was his magnificent depictions of the American West and the battle to win it, in films like *Stagecoach* (1939), *Fort Apache* (1947) and *Rio Grande* (1950), that ensured his lasting fame. Ford was sometimes accused of callousness in the way he portrayed the destruction of the native Americans. Late in life he rejected the charge, saying that the blood brothership he had sworn with various Indian nations meant more to him than his Oscars. 'Perhaps it's my Irish atavism, my sense of reality, of the beauty of clans, in contrast to the modern world . . . who better than an Irishman could understand the Indians, while being stirred by tales of the US Cavalry? We were on both sides of the epic.'

At the other end of the cinematic spectrum an Irish-German-American, Grace Kelly had established herself as the epitome of coolness and elegance in the 1950s. She was the daughter of Jack Kelly, a self-made millionaire through his building business who won an Olympic gold medal for rowing. He married Margaret Majer, who converted from Lutheranism to Catholicism to make the match. Grace was born in 1929. She was drawn to the theatre by her uncle, George Kelly, a Pulitzer prize winning dramatist, and after some Broadway roles made her Hollywood breakthrough playing a Quaker wife opposite Gary Cooper in *High Noon* (1952). Her career as an actress gave way to a second life as the wife of a minor royal figure, Prince Rainier of Monaco, who extracted a $2 million dowry from Jack Kelly as part of the arrangement. The deal was the wrong way round. It was clear that the builder's daughter from Philadelphia was the element of class in the equation, lending to the House of Grimaldi an undeserved lustre.

Ireland and Irishness were rarely treated with any seriousness in the movies. They were even more sentimentalized on television. A durable staple of popular entertainment were comedy shows depicting romance between Jewish boys and Irish girls. In reality, such matches were not common, a result of the prevailing relative religious strictness in both communities. That did not deter the authors of *Abie's Irish Rose*, which ran for 2,000 performances on Broadway in the 1920s or the makers of the twenty-two films about Jewish–Irish romances in the period. The formula still worked in the 1970s, 1980s and 1990s with television series like *Bridget Loves Bernie*, *Chicken Soup* and *Brooklyn Bridge*.

It was left to novelists to expose the dark reality of much of immigrant life. Irish writers, particularly from New York, revealed a world of alcoholism, violence and self-loathing that lay behind the bonhomous exterior presented in popular culture. In novels like Jimmy Breslin's *World without End, Amen* (1972) the cop hero bears little resemblance to the impassive stock figures of a thousand Hollywood dramas with their soft brogues and granite jaws, but is an alcoholic, tortured by an unhappy childhood, unfeeling teachers and a loveless marriage. In a later work, *Table Money*, set in Queens in the early 1970s, a good woman saves her Vietnam veteran husband from drink and the destructive macho culture his upbringing has imposed on him. One of the most gripping accounts of growing up poor in New York has been provided by Pete Hamill, the writer and journalist, in *A Drinking Life* (1993). It describes his relationship with his father Billy, a drunkard and a cripple who was incapable of demonstrating love. Despite the melancholy and bleakness of some of his home life Hamill writes about his upbringing with pride and affection, and acknowledges the decency of some of the values of Irish working-class society. His grandmother, a Catholic immigrant from Belfast, teaches him the lesson that 'Freedom is a lot more important than money . . . Remember that. Here we're free. And you must never be a bigot.'

The wearing of the green. A marcher in the annual New York St Patrick's Day Parade in 1996.

What is a bigot, young Hamill wants to know?

'"A bigot is a hater," she said. "A bigot hates Catholics. A bigot hates Jews. A bigot hates colored people. It's no sin to be poor . . . it *is* a sin to be a bigot."'

While there is a wealth of literature about the Irish American experience, there is a no such abundance of British Irish writing. Even though books, movies and drama by Irish writers about Irishness have never been more fashionable, this success has yet to manifest itself in a vogue for novels, films or plays that deal with the condition of Irish immigrants to Britain and their descendants.

It is hard not to see this as another manifestation of the profoundly different approach taken by the Irish in Britain and the Irish in America to the host nation. One simple comparison which makes the point is the relative ways in which St Patrick's Day is celebrated. From the time of the War of Independence the feast day has been marked with great fanfare in New York and the annual parade is one of the key events in the life of the city. The city comes to a standstill, and Americans who have never set foot in the Emerald Isle feel compelled to wear shamrocks and act as honorary Irishmen and women for the day. This is not an act of collective condescension but a genuine celebra-

The way it was. St Patrick's Day marchers parade through Manhattan on a dank spring day in 1919.

tion of Irish culture and achievement with which everyone, whether or not they have a drop of Irish blood in their veins, feels they can join in.

In London, by contrast, the feast day is barely celebrated at all, even though the Irish have been part of the social and economic fabric of the city for centuries. In recent years reticence about Irishness has diminished. But this development may well be part of a wider process of recognizing and celebrating ethnicity, of which the Irish are passive beneficiaries. The great London ethnic festival is the Notting Hill Carnival, a transplant from the Caribbean, which to some extent fulfils the same function as the St Patrick's Day Parade, but which celebrates a much later addition to the metropolitan racial smorgasbord.

The absence of ostentatious celebration of Irishness in Britain may in truth be a reflection of the fact that there is little to celebrate. The proximity of the real Ireland has served as a reminder of the failure of the state to provide all the Irish with a means of supporting themselves. In such circumstances displays of triumphalism might seem a little hollow. For the creation of the Irish state failed to halt the flow of Irishmen and women abroad. Many of the first to leave were Protestants escaping from real or perceived discrimination imposed by what threatened to be a quasi-confessional entity. The rest were the familiar columns of the young who reluctantly concluded that they would have to leave the homeland if they were to have any sort of life. When the 1931 census was taken the number of Irish born in England and Wales was found to be 381,089 compared with 364,749 in

Long before *Riverdance* these young members of the Dartford Irish Association (1962) were keeping the tradition of Irish dancing alive.

1920, the year before the Free State was founded. The outbreak of the Second World War brought restrictions on the movement of people from Eire, which had declared its neutrality in the conflict. Immigrants in Britain returned home. But acute labour shortages in the British wartime economy meant that the government was by 1942 issuing permits to Irish workers to fill the jobs of men off at the war. The construction boom that came with peace attracted building workers and about 100,000 people are estimated to have arrived in Britain from southern Ireland between 1946 and 1951 – including my mother, who came to work as a nurse. The immigration data for the period are patchy, but it is safe to say that a minimum of 30,000 Irish entered the country each year during the 1950s and settled.

The jobs to which the wartime and post-war Irish workers went were mainly the traditional ones – those that were too arduous, dirty or dangerous to appeal much to local workers. The 1961 census survey of the principal occupations of Irish-born males in Great Britain revealed that by far the biggest proportion – 19.5 per cent – worked as unskilled labourers. Only 6 per cent were classified as 'professional and technical'. The rest did a wide variety of mostly menial jobs. The situations-vacant columns of the *Dublin Evening Press* in July 1962 advertised posts in Britain for police constables and bar staff. Women were in demand as factory and canteen workers and domestic staff in hospitals. However, there was some migration of health professionals, attracted by the opportunities offered by the newly established National Health Service.

A sort of ghetto mentality persisted. The Catholic Irish tended to stick together, attend the same churches and send their children to the same schools, and first generation immigrants at least made an effort to perpetuate the culture they had left behind. Mary Hickman, an academic who specializes in the historical and contemporary experience of the Irish in Britain, remembers being sent to Irish dancing lessons. 'Every time we got together, whether it was for birthdays, marriages, funerals, christenings, whatever – there would be a big party and Irish songs would be sung and everyone would be singing or telling stories or trying to fix in your head which family tree you belonged to because you constantly forgot ... I took it completely for granted.'

The main instrument in maintaining identity was the Catholic Church. Mary Hickman calculates that, until the end of the 1970s, 70 per cent of Irish Catholics sent their children to denominational schools whether they themselves were practising or not. 'The evidence is that, regardless of their own habits of Mass attendance, the vast majority of Irish Catholic parents would not have sent their children to any but a Catholic school if one was available.' Children would travel long distances by public transport in order to attend.

The education on offer emphasized religious differences between Catholics and non-Catholics. But it did not suggest that these differences extended to political matters. Indeed the tone of the religious teaching to some extent promoted conservative values with a strong emphasis on obedience, continence and duty. At my own school, Wimbledon College, religion, or rather Catholicism, was omnipresent. Everything could be seen through the stained-glass filter provided by my Jesuit teachers. Catholicism had an opinion on everything. It went without saying that this point of view was superior to any other. The result was that pupils were imbued with a sense of exclusivity. The pupils at the neighbouring school may have been richer and their sports fields and laboratories better equipped. But they were hopelessly disadvantaged in one vital area. They were not members of the One Holy Catholic and Apostolic Church – a fact that their fancy bicycles and expensive rugby boots would never erase.

Women's work. An Irish woman graduate of the Lyons Private Catering School.

The message, not very subtly conveyed, was that Catholics were better than Protestants. If we learned that an actor or pop star or footballer was a member of the faith, their popularity soared. Yet despite encouraging this culture of superiority the fathers were anxious to inculcate respect for temporal authority and emphasize the need for loyalty to British institutions. The evidence of this was hanging on the walls of the college hall. Earlier in the century a number of boys had passed through the school who had gone on to distinguish themselves in Britain's wars. Two of them had won the highest award for gallantry, the Victoria Cross. Their portraits stared encouragingly down on us as we wolfed our dinners and rushed back into the playground to resume our games of English (never British for some reason) versus Germans.

Despite the fact that many of the boys and the priests and masters were of Irish stock, there was no attempt to promote Irish values or encourage interest in Irish history or current events. A few boys were forced by their parents to go Irish dancing or play the pipes. But this was considered a sissyish occupation and they were generally derided for doing so.

Whatever reinforcement of Irish culture there was came from home. But even there parents were fighting against hopeless odds. It was the post-Beatles era. The radio stations were full of brilliant British pop. The Irish had produced the Bachelors and Clodagh Rodgers. There was nothing particularly attractive about Ireland or Irishness. The stories and songs of our uncles and aunts seemed quaint, touching and slightly embarrassing. The place seemed moored in an unhappy past. We could not understand why anyone should want to cling so tenaciously to it.

This, in anecdotal form, is the background to a lapidary statement by Liam Ryan, who offers an explanation for the relative feebleness of Irish identity among the descendants of Irish immigrants. Surveying the Irish in Britain between the Second World War and 1990 he wrote:

> Irish assimilation into British society is among the fastest that occurs among immigrant groups anywhere in the world. Assimilation is practically complete in a single generation. The children of Irish immigrants, sometimes to the distress of their parents, grow up seeing themselves as English or Scots; they may acknowledge their Irish ancestry and exhibit a few inherited traits, but for all practical purposes they are indistinguishable from their British peers whether in respect of dress or in social, cultural or religious behaviour.

Professor Akenson speculates that the single biggest agency of Irish assimilation has been marriage. Data on marriage patterns that became available for the first time in 1970 suggested that 48 per cent of Irish-born males who married in England and Wales did not have Irish wives. The figure for Irishwomen marrying non-Irish husbands was 46 per cent. Extrapolating from these figures it is easy to see how Irishness could be bred out of a family in a very few generations.

Attempts have been made to suggest that anti-Irish prejudice and hostility on the part of the British may have encouraged the Irish to seek assimilation. Prejudice is notoriously difficult to quantify. Nonetheless it is true to say that the predominant stereotypes of Irish behaviour among the British remained depressingly current until

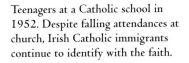

Teenagers at a Catholic school in 1952. Despite falling attendances at church, Irish Catholic immigrants continue to identify with the faith.

very recently, portraying Irishmen as comically stupid and perpetually drunk. An upwardly mobile first generation immigrant might strive hard to avoid such categorization by adopting self-consciously English middle-class behaviour. His sons and daughters, making their way in the world, would certainly be unlikely to see much advantage in emphasizing an Irishness they probably felt only residually if at all. But it is surely the overwhelming power and attraction of the host culture that ensured that a distinct and vigorous Irish subculture could not survive without a steady stream of incoming immigrants to sustain it.

The fact of assimilation means that the progress and achievements of the Irish in Britain are particularly hard to measure. A prominent man or woman may have an Irish name. But their bloodline may be so diluted as to make their ethnicity purely notional. The defining factor becomes whether they feel themselves to be Irish.

Perhaps the curious invisibility of the British Irish is an indication that they have achieved an anonymity which may be part of the emigrant impulse. By leaving your homeland, you are getting away from something. Certainly there has been little attempt by the Irish in Britain to identify themselves publicly with Irish causes. The long, slow slaughter in Northern Ireland has failed to produce any dynamic popular movement to resolve the situation, and any sympathies felt in the Irish community have been largely internalized. At the national level a few politicians of Irish origin have taken a special interest in the Northern Ireland troubles, but their contributions have not been remarkable or productive. When the former leader of the Greater London Council, Ken Livingstone, allied himself with Sinn Fein and attempted to link the issue with the plight of the working-class Irish in the metropolis he was accused of political opportunism and giving aid and comfort to terrorists.

The difference in the experiences of Irish emigrants to America and Britain in some ways seems to be a matter of geography, or rather proximity, as well as local social and political conditions. Far away from the homeland, resigned to the fact that the separation was probably final, the Irish American could nonetheless dream of home and cling to an identity which provided him with a social and emotional support system in alien territory. The guiding ethos and multi-ethnic nature of emergent America condoned such identification, as long as it did not supersede loyalty to the United States itself. In Britain there was no such luxury. To the Irish in Britain, Ireland was real, a place that no matter how much they were attached to it had to some extent let them down. To return to it could be a mark of success, but equally of failure. All in all, it was better not to dream dreams.

The original Irish theme pub. The subterranean fug of Ward's Irish House beneath Piccadilly Circus in its 1950s heyday.

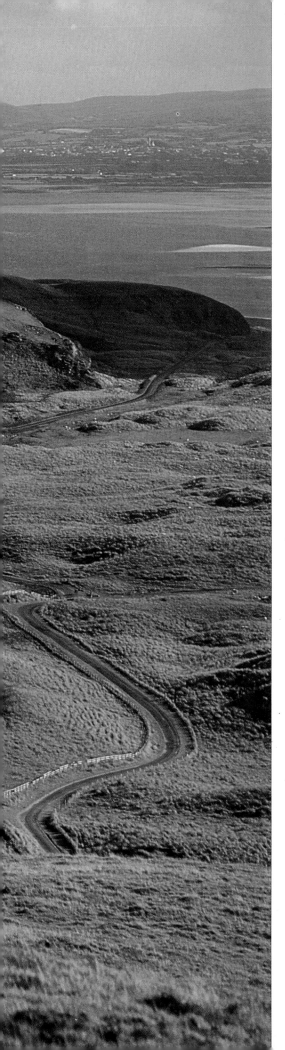

· 12 ·
EXILE AND OPPORTUNITY

E MIGRATION MEANT LOSS, dislocation, exile. It also meant freedom, opportunity, fulfilment. To those leaving, and to those they left behind, it meant, above all, a devastating sense of bereavement at the moment of departure. In the realist novelist Liam O'Flaherty's fictional account of an American wake he describes Mary and Michael taking their farewells of their parents, family and friends before setting off across the Atlantic. Confronted with the sight of her son and daughter standing silently and solemnly in their Sunday best, their mother breaks down.

> She burst into tears wailing: 'My children, oh, my children, far over the sea you will be carried, from me, your mother.' And she began to rock herself and she threw her apron over her head.

Immediately the cabin was full of the sound of bitter wailing. A dismal cry rose from the women gathered in the kitchen. 'Far over the sea they will be carried,' began woman after woman, and they all rocked themselves and hid their heads in their aprons.
When it was time to go,

> Mary and Michael got to their feet. Their father sprinkled them with holy water and they crossed themselves. Then, without looking at their mother, who lay in the chair with her hands clasped on her lap, looking at the ground in a silent, tearless stupor, they left the room ...
> As Michael was going out the door he picked a piece of loose whitewash from the wall and put it in his pocket. The

(Left) The green remembered hills: Donegal. *(Right)* The pain of departure was recorded in poem and song.

The last farewell. (Painting by James Fagan, 1853)

people filed out after them, down the yard and on to the road, like a funeral procession. The mother was left in the house with little Thomas and two old peasant women from the village. Nobody spoke in the cabin for a long time.

The sense of loss could be balanced by expectation of the good, bright life that lay ahead. But inevitably, for many, a mass of disappointment was in store, as Seamus O' Muircheartaigh's verse mournfully expresses:

> I got a letter from a relation
> Telling me to hasten across the sea
> That gold was to be found in plenty there
> And that I'd never have a hard day or a poor one again ...
>
> Naively I went abroad
> With my bag on my shoulder, praying to God
> To bring me safe to land through storm and wind
> Where I'd be a gentleman for the rest of my days
>
> Alas, when I landed
> I made for the city without delay
> But I never saw gold on the street corners
> Alas, I was a poor aimless person cast adrift.

Even those with less grandiose expectations than the disappointed emigrant of the poem, circumstances were very often hard and there were many sighing reflections in emigrant writings as to whether the new life was any better than the one they had left behind. As time passed the old country was inevitably idealized. The slum cabins and muddy roads became, in the distant imagination, white-washed cottages and stony boreens stretching out to green hills over which the rain is always curiously absent. Some, like Patrick Kane exiled in America from his boyhood Clare, dreamed of home but realized

> that all is now altered,
> My friends and companions are gone,
> That home is replaced by another,
> Beside which the Shannon rolls on;
> And if I should revisit that Island,
> That cottage which once I called home,
> There is none who would now recognize me,
> A stranger around there I'd roam.

John Archer Jackson records that a retired sailor, interviewed by a researcher in a London slum in the 1890s, was asked: 'Why do you stay in such a miserable hovel as this, when there is land and enough to spare in England, and especially in old Ireland, your native country where you might get a cot, or build one yourself, and a piece of land to cultivate, at less rent than the amount of your pension?'

'Arrah, mister, it's a long toime since I left Ireland and the old woman is here, and many old friends about …'

'The old woman of whom you spoke, your wife?'

'Sure no, me old mother it is that I'd be looking after.'

Memory tended to filter out the grimness of daily life back in Ireland.

Homesickness runs a deep, melancholy course through much emigrant writing, even down to the present day, afflicting the young emigrant in Ralph McTell's song *It's a Long Way from Clare to Here*.

Four who shared this room and we were caught up in the crack
Sleeping late on Sundays and we never got to Mass

When Friday comes around we're only into fighting
My ma would like a letter home but I'm too tired for writing

It almost breaks my heart when I think of my family
I told them I'd be coming home with my pockets full of green

The only time I feel alright is when I'm into drinking
It can sort of ease the pain of it and it levels out my thinking

I sometimes hear the fiddles play, maybe it's just a notion
I dream I see white horses dance upon that other ocean

There were two fundamental ways of dealing with homesickness and melancholy. You could get on with life. Or you could succumb. Much has been made of the prevalence of criminality, drunkenness and mental illness among Irish immigrants. Agreement will never be reached on whether these conditions were caused, or exacerbated, by the experience of immigration. Whether or not the Irish drink and fight more than any other nation is a question that can never be answered satisfactorily. What statistical evidence exists suggests that they were no more criminal than any other immigrant group. As Professor Akenson notes, 'being locked up relatively often is one of the prices a group pays for moving to a new country'. Young men everywhere — and most of the immigrants were young — tend to drink and fight. The interesting point is that the Irish were popularly supposed to be particularly prone to such behaviour.

On the question of mental illness, there seems to be powerful proof that immigrants are disproportionately afflicted, especially Irish ones. Alan M. Kraut's study of medical care among Irish immigrants in the nineteenth century shows that in New York three-quarters of admissions to the city's lunatic asylum on Blackwell's Island between 1849 and 1859 were immigrants and two-thirds of those were Irish. Both Irishmen and Irishwomen were reported as being susceptible to schizophrenia and alcohol-related syndromes after immigration. One physician observed that young women arrivals seemed especially prone to mental illness. He ascribed it to the 'combined moral and physical influences of their leaving the homes of their childhood, their coming almost destitute to a strange land, and often after great suffering'.

All immigrant groups to Australia in the late nineteenth century had insanity rates that were roughly five times higher than those of the native-born. The Irish had the worst. In 1900–1, when the Irish made up less than 5 per cent of the Australian population, nearly one-fifth of the inmates of insane asylums in Victoria and New South Wales were Irish born.

The problem has persisted. Liam Greenslade, examining mental-hospital admissions in England and Wales in 1971 and 1981, has found that 'Irish people, from both the Republic and Northern Ireland, had and continue to have the highest rates of admission to mental hospital of any migrant or ethnic/racial group'. In particular, the rates for Irish-born women were the highest for all groups and double those for English-born women. Other research has found the same Irish over-representation in mental illness cases in New York State and Canada for the same period. It has been pointed out that the population of Ireland itself is particularly affected by mental illness. In the mid-1950s, it had the highest psychiatric hospitalization rate in the world. In 1971 the Republic of Ireland had double the schizophrenia rate normal for western societies. In spite of this, the incidence of mental illness among other immigrant groups suggests that the shock of exile must in at least some cases have played some part in contributing to mental illness and that the unscientific but kindly diagnosis of the New York physician was correct: for some, the experience of emigration was just too much.

Along with disorientation and hardship, the newcomers had to put up with prejudice. As we have seen, contempt for the Irish was institutionalized in America and Britain in the nineteenth century. A *Punch* cartoon of 1880 shows Uncle Sam and John Bull despairing of the behaviour of the Irish, who are represented by a squat, ape-like man dancing a jig and waving a knife in one hand and a shillelagh in the other. The cartoonist reflected the Darwinian controversy, suggesting that the Irish might provide a proof of the theory that man was descended from the ape. In America, an 1851 *Harper's Magazine* article on the 'Celtic Physiognomy' described two Irish newcomers as if they were interesting specimens recently arrived from the jungle and now at the local zoo: 'distinctly marked – the small and somewhat upturned nose, the black tint of the skin; the eyes now looking gray, now black; the freckled cheek and sandy hair. Beard and whiskers covered half the face, and short, square-shouldered bodies were bent forward with eager impatience.'

In America the social and political progress of the Irish made such characterizations unacceptable before the century was out. In Britain, though, prejudice against the Irish lingered longer. In the 1950s, the immigrant labourer could expect to be turned away by landladies operating a 'No Irish, No Coloureds' policy and to be viewed with automatic suspicion by the local police. The attitude of the chairman of the London Sessions in 1957 who declared that 'This court is infested with Irishmen who come here to commit offences and the more that can be persuaded to go back, the better' was not uncommon. The Irishman might get on well enough with his workmates at the site. But their attitude might well be tinged with condescension as he was expected to conform to the stereotype of over-fondness of drink and dim-wittedness. Such attitudes have changed considerably, as we shall see in the next chapter. But the knowledge that you are not wanted, in a place you may not have wanted to go to in the first place, is a peculiarly depressing revelation.

Despite all the undoubted pain of exile, emigration was for many a liberating and enriching experience, releasing able and energetic men and women from a life of penury, drudgery and intellectual and social confinement and ushering them into a world where they had the chance to be all they wanted to be. This was particularly true in the case of women, for whom life in Ireland, especially in the later nineteenth century, was bleak, often offering a choice between marriage to a much older man or spinsterhood and domestic semi-slavery ministering to a father and unmarried brothers.

The historian Hasia R. Diner has characterized the Irish exodus to America as 'a women's migration. Women outnumbered men as migrants. Within any family, daughters were more likely to migrate than sons. They were single. They weren't following husbands. They were brought to America by sisters, by female cousins, by female friends, by aunts ... in some ways, men were barely present.' She describes 'a typical story of a typical servant girl. She comes to America with a ticket sent to her by her sister. She has a job waiting for her, perhaps in the same home where her sister is employed, or perhaps that of the employer's daughter or neighbour. She lives in an American home, with a couple of other Irish girls with whom she shares a room. Over the course of five years she saves a certain amount of money, having first taken care of her obligations to her family back home. Then she gets married.'

Professor Diner's researches suggest that the girl would usually marry down, to an unskilled or semi-skilled labourer, who would bring nothing, financially, to the marriage. 'She was the one who brought the little fortune into the family and she was also the one who broadens the home and establishes American standards of dress, of cleanliness, of furnishing, of diet. She brought in an American standard by which she raised her children.'

Thus it was Irishwomen who in many cases laid the foundation block which the Irish climbed upon to hoist themselves out of the ghetto. Sons often followed their fathers' occupation, perhaps moving one notch up the scale from semi-skilled to get a proper trade. The women made a bigger social leap. The daughters of maids often became schoolteachers, nurses, stenographers, clerks, breaking into the white collar life of the office and its consequent status and associations of belonging to the great

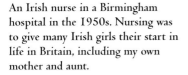

An Irish nurse in a Birmingham hospital in the 1950s. Nursing was to give many Irish girls their start in life in Britain, including my own mother and aunt.

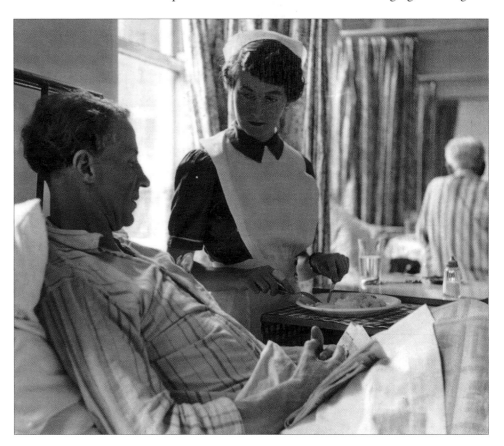

world and not just the ghetto. The servant girl, according to Diner, had 'a vision of making herself over in America, becoming economically independent, a person of value, a person worthy of respect and while she in her lifetime was not going to be able to move out of the working class, she invested that resource and that drive in her daughters, who are one of the great success stories of this kind of immigrant saga'.

Diner argues that in some ways men suffered more than women in the new world:

> The stories we have – of breakdowns, of alcoholism, of disillusionment, of dislocation, of being unable to fit in, of abandonment – were the stories of men. That is not to say that all men went through this. But those who did were more likely to be men than women. The men came from a society that valued men, and male activity in a male group and male achievement. They came into a place where it was their wives and their daughters and their sisters who were able to seize the initiative and who viewed themselves as the valued ones. For men this became a kind of double burden. Not only did the migration not achieve their goals but they saw their wives and the women in their community flourishing in a way they weren't supposed to.

Not only was the servant girl the springboard for social mobility abroad. She was also a vital cog in the economic machine of Ireland itself. One estimate in the 1870s calculated that a third of all the money circulating in Ireland was made up of remittances sent by Irish girls in the United States.

That money went to help the family buy a farm so they should not be at the whims of somebody else as landlord. It helped the family move out of a cabin into a house with a real roof. It helped a brother to get an education. It helped a sister who wanted to become a nun and needed a dowry to enter the convent. It helped another sister to migrate. They sent back money to the town to buy new bells for the church or to pay for a baptismal font or a new school . . . the development of Ireland was on the backs of Irish servant girls.

The picture was different in Britain, where Irish immigrant men outnumbered the females. The women tended to marry young and had no time to work independently and amass the nest egg that their counterparts in America were able to deploy so effectively. The result was that women in the Irish community were much more dominated by their menfolk and did not succeed in building up the networks of female support that buttressed much of Catholic Irish society in America.

The courage and enterprise of Irishwomen immigrants created a new Irish stereotype, this time a positive one. It was an image of an independent, feisty individual navigating a passage through life according to strictly fixed moral bearings, a loyal friend and a dangerous foe.

Irishwomen and their descendants rose to the top of the professions where they first made their mark, like education and medicine. The pervasiveness of their success is now so great that it would be artificial to single out an individual. The success of Irishwomen – and men – in America, Britain, Australia, New Zealand, South Africa – virtually everywhere they have gone, raises the question of what would have happened if circumstances had been different and the economic, social and political imperatives had never existed that created the exodus.

Ireland is a small country, whose geographical circumstances ensure that it must stay that way. It is an island, surrounded by seas, historically far from trade routes that might otherwise have afforded it the opportunity to achieve disproportionate wealth or power – that is, to be like Britain. Had fate and foreigners treated it more kindly it might have remained a dull, comfortable sort of place, unobtrusive, quietly prosperous, producing generations of stolid farmers and fishermen and tradespeople, a sort of Celtic Norway, respectable but uninspiring. On the other hand its people might have chafed at such an ordinary destiny and like the Prussians, citizens of another state with no extraordinary natural resources apart from its people, set about carving a bigger niche for their country in the world, one more in keeping with their own view of its importance.

In some ways, the latter course of action would seem more likely. The warrior tradition of the Celts was no balladeer's fantasy. Nor did the Irish ever lack any sense of self-esteem. Extreme boastfulness is one of the characteristics lampooned by the English in their endless satires of Irishry. A handbill that circulated in Liverpool in the nineteenth century tells the tale of an Irishman who goes into a barbershop while the barber is out and allows himself to be shaved by the owner's monkey with disastrous results. The injured party angrily declares himself to be 'a son of the great O'Callaghan, and brother of the great O'Brian. I am also related to all the O's in Ireland, by my mother's side of the house. Likewise to the family of the Fitzpatricks, which have been well known in Ireland for forty thousand years.' The man is in fact a seasonal labourer over for the harvest.

Such a people were unlikely to have been satisfied with the restrictive life and society that geographical circumstances forced upon them. Had Ireland achieved independence far earlier, its own government would have been answerable to a population seeking to satisfy its economic and political aspirations. Failure to do so might have produced an unhappy and unstable society. Alternatively, internal pressure might have produced a search for *Lebensraum*. In different circumstances Ireland might have become a bully nation, shaking down its neighbours to obtain the wherewithal to live in the manner to which it felt it should be accustomed.

History determined that it avoided that fate. By coming late to statehood, Ireland remained largely unbesmirched by the sins that inevitably accompany the exercise of power. At the same time its people were able to make their way in the world, satisfying their temporal ambitions while spreading Irish values by the peaceful means of example. The societies they were going to were Christian and capitalist. They had no shortage of faults. But, in the context of the times, they were open societies that allowed social mobility and economic progress, and even fame, to those with sufficient energy, skill and luck. Without emigration the Ulsterman Thomas Mellon would never have founded one of the world's great fortunes or John L. Sullivan, the 'Boston strongboy', become the best known boxer of his day. Very few achieved riches or celebrity in any of the places where they fetched up. But sufficient did so for the rest to know that it was a possibility. And their failure to achieve great things was due to a lack of ambition or a lack of ability rather than because society was arranged to prevent them doing so.

The metaphor of emigration as liberation is particularly appropriate in the case of Irish writers. So marked was the tradition of exile that to stay at home was to invite obscurity. The case of the most famous literary émigré, James Joyce, in some ways closely parallels the experience of all emigrants. Joyce's departure was strictly voluntary but in a sense it was imposed on him by the intellectual limitations of a small and often small-minded place. In exile, though, thoughts of Ireland sustained and inspired him, notably in *Ulysses* (1922). Without Ireland, there would have been no James Joyce. Yet it was equally clear that he could not have lived there, especially in the parochial, pietist climate that descended on the land after the foundation of the Free State, as power moved into the hands of a narrow-minded political class steeped in rural values. Joyce was appalled to hear of the censorship regime imposed by the new authorities which meant that any work could be banned once a citizen had lodged a complaint with a board of moral guardians, charging that it advocated immorality or artificial birth control or some such. The Dublin of his youth, he told a visitor in Paris, was much more free and easy. 'There was a kind of desperate freedom which comes from a lack of responsibility, for the English were in governance then, so everyone said what he liked.'

The paradox that under the farmers and bureaucrats who ran the Free State there was less freedom than before caused other intellectuals like George Russell and Thomas MacGreevey to leave. The most prominent exile after Joyce was Samuel Beckett, who made the eccentric decision to leave Ireland for France in 1939, just as a German invasion looked imminent, telling his family that he would rather live in a France at war than an Ireland at peace. Despite the fact that he chose to write henceforth in French much of his work has recognizably Irish characters drawn from an ancient Irish literary tradition. In their social lives, Joyce and Beckett both attempted to recreate the intimacy of Irish social life, appearing at a certain bar, in Beckett's case the Falstaff in Montparnasse, at a certain hour to rendezvous with a regular coterie to drink and gossip, telling and retelling the same stories over and over. This was not the Rive Gauche of Sartre and De Beauvoir but an attempt to reproduce the ambience of a Dublin pub.

The societies to which the emigrants went were overwhelmingly English speaking, a fact which in a country like America paradoxically helped the Irish to preserve a distinct subculture. In the case of Argentina, where Irish settlers arrived in considerable numbers in the nineteenth century, it was necessary ultimately to speak Spanish to survive. Despite the best efforts of the likes of Fr Anthony Fahy, who energetically served as chaplain to the Irish community, the Irish identity had been swallowed up in the surrounding cultural sea in four generations.

Most Irish emigrants, then, arrived with a great advantage over other emigrant groups. Unlike the Germans and Italians reaching America in great waves from Europe in the nineteenth century, or the Russian Jews arriving in London, they could

James Joyce loitering outside Shakespeare and Company in Paris in 1938 on what, despite his overcoat, looks like a hot summer's day. The woman with him is Adrienne Monnier.

The playwright and author Brendan Behan in characteristic surroundings in a Dublin pub. What is uncharacteristic is the modest half pint of stout in his hand.

speak the local language. This gave them a potential entry into the world of official employment. The biggest and most welcoming employer, in the case of Britain, was undoubtedly the armed services. The presence of Irishmen in the ranks of the British army and navy has been one of the great constants of military history. The Irish Brigades fighting in the service of France against the British, often to their dismay, found themselves pitched against their own countrymen. This fact has been a source of embarrassment, not to say shame, among Irish writers who have chosen to interpret it as yet another humiliation visited on patriotic Irishmen by the Saxon foe. The nineteenth-century writer and activist John Denvir noted that 'in the British army and in the police force there have been men, mostly compelled by adverse circumstances, who have for a time worn the blue, or the green or the scarlet coat of Britain without changing the Irish heart beneath'.

We have seen how the Irish swarmed into the ranks of the police forces of the East Coast cities of America, and were also prominent in the US military. Joining the armed ranks of the establishment posed no great ideological problem in America. It was work, not particularly well paid but certainly secure, offering prospects and political connections. This was not the case in Britain. Taking the king's or queen's shilling ran counter to the bitter anti-English ethos that veined Irish folk memories and folk culture. It is possible that the Irishman signing up was able to dislocate his actions in just the way that Denvir describes, regarding it as a purely mercenary arrangement. That is how the British seemed to see it. The *Westminster Review* in 1835 remarked on the number of Irish in the armed forces at the time, observing that 'Irishmen may freely man our navy, or serve in our armies, because we do not desire that employment for ourselves. It is more problematical whether they may officer them, because that is more genteel and lucrative, and should therefore be reserved for ourselves.'

The British army at various times in the nineteenth century had a staggeringly high proportion of Irish. In 1841, when the Irish population was 32.3 per cent of that of the United Kingdom, 42.2 per cent of the army was Irish. The figure goes into a slow decline but even at the end of the century nearly one in five of British soldiers was Irish born. Add to that the second generation Irishmen who must have been in the ranks and their presence becomes very significant. Thus, amid the red-coated figures, stoically standing back to back and discharging their rifles into the advancing hordes of Pathans, Zulus and Fuzzy-Wuzzies, there were any number of Kellys and Burkes and Sheas, shoring up the Empire that denied them their liberty at home. During the First World War, 140,000 Irish men volunteered for the British forces, of whom about 65,000 were Catholics.

Interestingly the Irish make only rare individual appearances in the barrack room ballads of the bard of Empire, Rudyard Kipling. In the poem 'Belts', an Irish regiment and an English cavalry regiment set about each other in a drunken punch-up in Dublin.

> There was a row in Silver Street – they sent the Polis there
> The English were too drunk to know, the Irish didn't care;
> But when they grew impertinent we simultaneous rose
> Till half o' them was Liffey mud and half was tatthered clo'es.

The brawl ends in tragedy when one of the Irishmen gets stabbed to death. It is a curiously undramatic poem that seems to lack a point. What is interesting is the very ordinariness of the coexistence of an Irish and an English regiment, fighting among themselves in the same sort of way as a group of Paras and Marines might if they encountered each other in a pub today.

In the mid-Victorian period some 40 per cent of the Irish in the ranks had signed up in England or Scotland. In all likelihood that means that they had come to Britain as economic migrants, failed to make their way and enlisted for a roof over their head and a weekly wage. The main motivation, then, would appear to be mercenary. Historians have coined a rather unkind term for this kind of person – 'prefabricated

Irish Guards in the mud and desolation of Ypres during the First World War.

collaborator'. It may perhaps be more justly applied to the Irish who joined the colonial administration service, where the relationship to and identification with the imperial and colonial mission was inescapable. 'The empire', Professor Akenson has noted, 'was full of them.' One-third of the United Kingdom governors of South Africa were Irish, as were many of its judges and middle-level officials. In India, after entry into the civil service became competitive in 1855 the proportion of Irish jumped dramatically from about 5 per cent between 1809 and 1850 to 24 per cent by 1863. The numbers began to drop thereafter when the authorities, alarmed by the influx of Irish graduates, rigged the entry process against them. Many of these Irishmen were Protestant. But a significant and growing number were Catholic. In the administrative grades of the Indian civil service only 8 per cent of recruits were Catholic in the years 1855–64. By the period 1905–14 this figure had reached 29 per cent. Akenson points out that such participation was a logical extension of what was happening in Ireland itself. After Catholic emancipation Catholics began to be employed in Irish civil service departments to the point in 1911 when they held 60 per cent of all posts.

Their presence in the ranks of the colonial service suggests a somewhat greater commitment to imperialism. A student of the phenomenon, Scott B. Cook, has written that, of Irish responses to imperialism, 'one of the most common, contrary to what most of the historical literature has stressed, was that of support'. By that he means 'a broad category encompassing conscious and active collaboration as well as acquiescence in laws, values, and social structures that were partly shaped by British hegemony'.

Playing the game. Irish serviceman hockey players in Delhi, 1921.

The Irish showed, then, that they could be as good imperialists as the British. All they lacked was an empire of their own. By the end of the twentieth century it is arguable that they have one. It does not have neatly defined boundaries and requires no army, navy or air force to defend it. Its visible representatives are not merely politicians but rock stars, writers, poets, film directors and actors. Behind them stands a vast horde of nameless men and women, who set off from their little island homes and crossed hostile seas to inhospitable shores equipped in most cases with little more than a strong back, a willingness to work and a determination to survive. From these fundamental resources the Irish have built a conceptual domain that looks set to prove more enduring than the Empire that oppressed them for so long. The story of emigration was a long, painful, harrowing saga of suffering and loss, but it has a triumphant and happy ending. Emigration gave Ireland to the world.

Life in the Raj. A surprising number of Irishmen and women served it loyally.

Epilogue

Just before Christmas in 1998 British newspapers carried a photograph of a woman vagrant being carried out of a London Underground station and dumped in the street with the rubbish. The accompanying stories laboriously pointed out the gap between the actions of the London Transport staff and the generosity of spirit that was supposed to prevail during the season of goodwill. The tramp in question was identified only as Tessy. She lived rough, suffered from epilepsy and was practically crippled from a broken pelvis sustained in a fall. She was, the newspapers reported, Irish and an alcoholic.

One can imagine the unease of the homeward-bound young accountants and managers, natives of Dublin and Cork and Limerick, reading the story in the Tube or crammed into the Docklands Light Railway as it jerked its spasmodic way from the glittering capitalist monolith of Canary Wharf in East London to the centre of town. The contrast between the image of Irishness evoked by poor Tessy and their own smooth, confident selves could not be more marked. She was their sort of age — thirty-three — but inhabited an entirely different universe to that of the new breed of Irish professionals blazing a trail through London, Brussels and New York.

Far more in keeping with the ethos of the new generation of Irish was another story which appeared a few weeks later. This time the subject was a sixteen-year-old Irish schoolgirl, Sarah Flannery, who had been hailed as a mathematical genius after devising a code for sending encrypted computer messages that allowed confidential information to be transmitted by e-mail. The report said she had been inundated with offers of jobs and scholarships from international computer companies

(*Left*) The next generation. Irish schoolchildren in the gallery of the Dublin stock exchange. (*Above*) Temple of capitalism: London's Canary Wharf.

and universities. The tone of *The Times* report was instructive. There was no element of surprise that Ireland should have produced such a prodigy. Somehow her success seemed part of an established phenomenon, another proof that Ireland was a dynamic nation, singularly well fitted to deal with the challenges of the technological age.

Just as Ireland has changed, so has the character of the people it exports. In the 1980s and 1990s the nature, and by extension the image, of Irish immigrants underwent a transformation. Previously, on arrival in a new country, the Irish had taken their place on the lower slopes of the labour market, in jobs that locals were unwilling, on account of conditions or wages, to do. It would be an over-simplification to say that a yuppie generation completely replaced the traditional ranks of unskilled and semi-skilled migrants. Nonetheless, many of the new arrivals were now starting halfway to the summit of achievement, propelled upwards by a mastery of contemporary skills that made them attractive to modern employers.

The army of young professionals was in part a consequence of government policies which altered Ireland deeply in the 1960s, turning it into a society that, while remaining deeply conservative in social matters, understood and embraced many aspects of the coming hi-tech era. The strategy was set by Sean Lemass's Programme for Economic Expansion of 1958, whose free trade policies encouraged foreign capital investment in Ireland and created jobs. Much of the new industry was hi-tech, foreign owned and export oriented. The resultant economic growth created a boom in the 1970s. The plan left many economic problems — such as the continuing weakness of indigenous industry — unaddressed, and the flaws in it were to be exposed cruelly in the following decade.

Nevertheless, the 1970s will always be remembered in Ireland for one extraordinary fact. For the first time since anyone could remember more people came in to Ireland than left it. Between 1971 and 1979, there was a sustained net inflow of population. The fact is all the more impressive when it is remembered that these were the darkest years of the Troubles, rumbling ominously north of the border in the six counties. By the end of the decade, Ireland had the fastest economic growth of any member of the European Community. As academic Linda Dowling Almeida puts it, 'the future looked bright for the country. Its young people were arguably the best educated generation it had ever produced.' For a while it seemed that a great watershed had been reached in the nation's history. For the first time, young people would not have to move abroad to have a happy, fulfilled life.

But it was not to be. The world recession of 1979–80 had a drastic effect on Ireland. It had borrowed and spent heavily to pay for growth, and debt now hobbled its chances of recovery. The new decade was a period of inflation, high unemployment and a sort of social loss of innocence which saw drugs and crime invade the poorer parts of Dublin. Inevitably, emigration resumed. Between 1981 and 1990, the country experienced a total net population loss of 208,000. In one year alone – 1988–9 – 46,000 people left. Most of them,

The outrages of the IRA have somehow failed to dent the positive image of the Irish.

Protestant Loyalists marching in the early days of the Troubles.

about 70 per cent, went to Britain. An unknown number went to America. Changes in US immigration law focusing on family reunion criteria rather than national origins made immigration more difficult for the Irish and other western Europeans to enter the country legally. Most of them arrived as tourists or temporary workers, staying on after their visas ran out.

The Irish also established themselves in Europe, particularly in Brussels, the home of European government. Once again, Irish politicians were prescient in spotting the potential of the Common Market and early on were eager to leapfrog Britain and plunge into the political and economic opportunities the European project offered to a small, poor country. They proved particularly adept at exploiting agricultural subsidies and development funds, which transformed the national infrastructure. But beyond that they established themselves as enthusiastic Europeans whose positive attitude was a welcome contrast to the hesitancy, suspicion and intermittent hostility displayed by the British.

As the century drew to a close young Irishwomen and men seemed more inclined to seek their fortunes in Britain and Europe than in the United States. There were practical reasons for this. America's doors were no longer open to the Irish. Irish politicians had to go to humiliating lengths to lobby the American authorities to show leniency to the army of undocumented immigrants living illegally in the country and allow them to stay on. In some ways the life of the illegals – the New Irish, as they styled themselves – was a throwback to the early days of the influx. The

Modern Dublin: a fashionable city.

newcomers were mostly young and single. Their precarious status condemned them to a marginal existence in which they could not exploit their educations and skills and which forced them to work on the edge of the economy as barmen, nannies and waitresses. Like their nineteenth-century predecessors, they huddled together for social and economic warmth and security, clustering in communities in Queens and the Bronx. They spent a lot of time in the pub. A survey by Linda Dowling Almeida conducted at the end of the 1980s showed that 65 per cent said that hanging around bars was their main leisure activity. Their testimony is suffused with the same melancholy that echoes down to us from the writings of the early emigrants, far from home with no way back. 'What's the point [of going home to Cavan]?' asked one interviewee in a New Jersey suburb. 'You go back looking for people and then you realize they're probably living only 100 miles from you here. You start looking for them. They're in New York, they're in London, they're in Canada. They're all gone.'

The subsequent regularization of the position of thousands of illegals created a climate of security in which the New Irish, like their antecedents, quickly found their feet. A writer, Ray O'Hanlon, who had himself emigrated to New York from Dublin in 1987, has identified the phenomenon of the transatlantic immigrant, who exploits ease of communications and computer technology to keep a foot in both camps. 'It is now possible', he declares, 'to re-emigrate "home" while, in some cases, never fully forsaking New York. There are not a few New York Irish who have returned to Ireland while leaving a business up and running in Queens, the Bronx, or Yonkers.'

At the time of writing Ireland is again undergoing a boom that has once more reversed the emigration trend, with immigrants exceeding emigrants by 22,800 in 1998. Once again the Irish economy is billed as the 'fastest growing in Europe' with growth rates reaching 9 per cent. Prosperity is being measured by the dubious yardstick of rocketing house prices, which rose nationally by 27.8 per cent in 1998 and in Dublin and the surrounding counties of Kildare, Louth, Meath and Wicklow by an astonishing 44 per cent. Expatriates returning home for Christmas discovered the job market was so buoyant that they were able to sign up and stayed on.

This resourcefulness, flexibility and ability to exploit innovation and take chances are testimony to the fact that many of those who left and are leaving are the cream of the country. In the 1980s an estimated 25 per cent of graduates went abroad seeking new opportunities. Mostly they were well armed with the qualifications needed to survive in the contemporary job market, a result of the dramatic changes rapid industrialization has wrought in Irish society since the 1950s, which meant that social standing was no longer based on family property but on skills and education. Education was to some extent geared to the needs of the foreign industries now planted around the land. Successive governments' understanding of the importance of Europe encouraged an emphasis on language skills, putting Irish school-leavers and graduates way ahead of their largely monoglot competitors across the sea in Britain. Thus many of those seeking work abroad were coming from a position of strength, and another departure from the past — from an urban background which had conditioned them to city life.

The fact that emigration is still a central feature of Irish life continues to rankle with some, who see it as ongoing proof of the failure of the Irish nation to achieve proper statehood. What kind of country, after all, can feel comfortable with itself for persistently failing to keep its young at home? But the impulses of emigration have changed. The force driving the young professionals and managers abroad is not survival but success. A survey by Gerald Hanlon of exiled young professionals reveals that while most of them could have stayed on in Ireland making a reasonable living they still decided to emigrate. 'They leave because their career paths are international,' he concludes. 'To fulfil their professional aspirations they must go where multinationals have established their headquarters or certain key sites … Ireland as a small peripheral economy is simply not suitable for such sites.'

In this respect the young Irish were only doing what ambitious young people were doing all over the world. At the time, in the 1980s, British men and women had to look abroad if they had their eyes fixed seriously on the big prizes – to New York and Hong Kong, for example if they worked in the financial sector. Later, in the 1990s, the European Union concept of a truly free continental job market was moving close to a reality as young French graduates flocked to London to escape their own enfeebled economy and to get a slice of the mini-boom that buoyed Britain up at the end of the decade.

With their skills and attitude the Irish are already at an advantage in the contemporary job market. With their tradition of emigration, of moving where the jobs and the opportunities are, there is an extra keenness to their competitive edge. A German study noted by Ellen Hazelkorn forecast for Europe an increase of 3.4 million jobs in highly skilled occupations and a loss of 2 million unskilled and low-skilled jobs by the year 2010. At the same time the pool of young, educated labour required to fill them is falling. However, 28 per cent of the Irish population at the start of the 1990s was under fifteen. Thus it looks inevitable that emigration will continue to be a fact of Irish life, well into the twenty-first century.

It is possible to put too rosy a gloss on the life of the new emigrants. There are familiar, ugly outcrops of fact that poke through the sunny landscape. A report in the *British Journal of Psychiatry* in 1998 on the mental state of the estimated 2.5 million Irish living in Britain states that Irish immigrants suffered poorer physical and mental health, experienced higher levels of alcohol abuse and had a higher rate of suicide than any other racial minority in the country. Irish people were the only immigrant group whose life expectancy declined on arrival in Britain. Irishmen were nine times as likely to suffer from alcohol-related disorders than their British counterparts and were two and a half times more prone to depression. They were more than 50 per cent more likely to commit suicide. It was not only first-generation migrants who were affected. The sons and daughters of immigrants suffered a far higher mortality rate than their native British counterparts.

These findings would seem to suggest that the image of the Irish immigrant, morose, turning to the bottle to assuage his melancholy and dislocation, by no means belongs to the past. But it is a picture that no one is interested in. The positive aspects of Irishness have now almost completely overwhelmed negative images of wildness and incontinence. The fondness for drink which so appalled moralizing

One of the great pubs of Ireland, the Crown Bar in Belfast.

English observers is celebrated in the onward march of the Irish pub, which has penetrated virtually every corner of the globe. It is now possible, in any major and many minor cities in the world, to walk into a smoky bar on a Friday night, hung with road signs telling how far it is to Ballyhooly or Kiltimagh, and watch men in suits desperately trying to get their vocal chords round the component parts of the word 'Guinness'. Irishness is associated with fun, creativity, good-heartedness and tolerance. It is one of the great triumphs of the Irish that they have established this reputation at the same time as the IRA has rooted itself in the global psyche as one of the world's most efficient and ruthless practitioners of terror.

The positive image has been reinforced by a great flowering of Irish artistic talent in films, literature and music. Distinctly Irish movie-makers like Neil Jordan, the great poet Seamus Heaney, novelists like Paddy Doyle and rock bands like U2 have hoisted Ireland to the top of the peaks of the Parnassus of contemporary fame. Ireland, and being Irish, is cool, possibly for the first time ever.

The novelist Joseph O'Connor, who was born in 1963, grew up imagining that Ireland had no links with the outside world. 'The Republic of Ireland was missing from the weather map in the British newspapers and Northern Ireland was transformed into a little island. Bands never came here and films were never made here. You accepted that you lived in nowhere land.' O'Connor left Ireland along with 70,000 others in 1986 and launched his literary career in London. His first novel, *Cowboys and Indians*, was about leaving. His third, *The Salesman*, is set in Ireland – he has moved back, at least partly, dividing his time between Dublin and London.

O'Connor says contemporary Irish writers are possibly the first not to be decisively influenced by the preceding generation and by the fact of their own Irishness.

Ersatz antiquity in a theme pub in London.

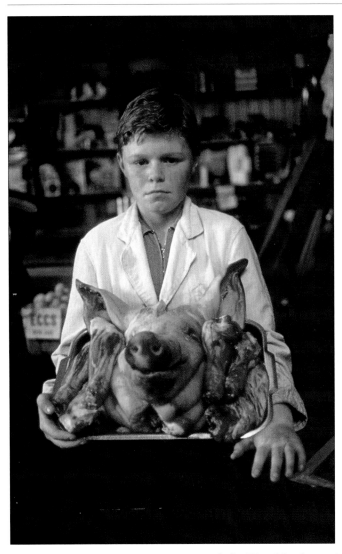

Neil Jordan's *The Butcher Boy*, based on Patrick McCabe's novel, is a typical contemporary Irish arts success story.

The influences and themes are European or American. 'There are fewer Irish novels with crucifixes in them.' His contemporaries are writers first and Irish second. The contemporary vibrancy of the Irish scene is in a way coincidental. Talent has been globalized, like everything else.

Ireland's current coolness may be news to the drinkers in a Kilburn pub, or the digger driver scooping out the foundations of the new Berlin. By the time they become acquainted with this surprising new development, the moment may have passed. Fashion is too fickle an instrument with which to test progress. What is more interesting and more significant is that the Irish have become ordinary. Their places at the bottom of the social ladder have for some time now been occupied by other groups, first by West Indian and Asian immigrants from the vanished British Empire, then by economic refugees seizing the chance afforded by the collapse of communism to head west in search of the holy grails of the emigrant: prosperity, opportunity, freedom. They are indistinguishable from the white people around them by their religion or politics. Catholicism no longer carries any stigma – if anything, the reverse is true. The Church of Rome is perceived as having an admirable vigour and doctrinal consistency when contrasted with the hesitancy and eagerness to please that seems to afflict the Church of England. Politically, the Irish are unremarkable. Whatever passions the issue of the North may have aroused at the beginning of the Troubles have since died down. War weariness and boredom mean that the Irish are as eager for a solution as any Briton, and probably as unconcerned with the fine detail of the settlement.

Ireland's relative prosperity has meant that it too is now a target for immigrants, particularly the huddled masses of economic refugees of which its population until so recently formed a part. The reaction of the country to this development provides perhaps the ultimate proof of how ordinary Ireland has become. During the late 1990s emigrants from eastern Europe and Africa began arriving illegally at air and sea ports in the Republic, often claiming to be political refugees seeking asylum from oppressive regimes. After centuries in the role of supplicant, Ireland found itself playing the part of seigneur. It would be nice to report that the long centuries in which emigration had been a central fact of Irish life had equipped Ireland with a particular sensibility when it came to dealing with the problem. That is not how it turned out. The Irish media and Irish authorities reacted with the same stern pragmatism as every government faced with the prospect of an alien influx. Legislation was prepared to fine employers large sums for employing illegal immigrant labour and to threaten jail sentences for truck drivers and transport companies found to be carrying asylum seekers.

Ireland, then, can be said to have finally taken its place amid the ranks of first-world countries. It no longer needs anyone's compassion or condescension. Emigration, for so long a shaming badge of the country's inability to support itself, has become something else entirely. Increasingly it is being seen as a measure of the tremendous wealth of Ireland's human resources. Brian Lenihan, the sometime Irish foreign minister, had this in mind when he said: 'What we have now is a very literate emigrant who thinks nothing of coming to the United States and going back to Ireland and maybe on to Germany and back to Ireland again … the world is now one world and they can always return to Ireland with the skills they have developed. We regard them as part of a global generation of Irish people. We shouldn't be defeatist or pessimistic about it. We should be proud of it. After all, we can't all live on a small island.'

So, as the new millennium opens, the great rhythms of the story of Irish emigration might seem to have etched a huge circle in the surface of history. Like their Celtic missionary and trader forebears, the Irish are making their way in the world on equal terms, full of pride and confident in the belief that they are enriching the societies they adopt and being enriched in return. In a way the world has caught up with them. Once upon a time it was only the poor and the religiously and politically oppressed who were impelled to consider exile as a life choice. Now, the internationalization of life means that more and more of us are forced to do so.

The great difference between the old emigrants and their young descendants is that for the new generation emigration no longer means exile. The last wave at the departure gates as the son or daughter sets off for London or Brussels or Paris or New York has none of the heartbreaking poignancy of the nineteenth-century American wake. The departed will come back – perhaps for good, if they want to. Parents and children are separated by no more than a few hours' flying time.

To that extent, emigration has lost its epic dimensions. The old exiles were leaving behind everything, family, friends, the landscape and patterns of life that meant so much to them. It is a tribute to their fortitude that they were able to achieve so much in strange and often hostile new homes. The resulting construct is unique: a cultural, economic and political universe built on the talent and energy that the emigrants were unable to expend at home. It was built without bloodshed, without oppression or dispossession or any of the other inevitabilities of expansion and conquest. But there it stands, while more visible dominions have crumbled and decayed, truly the sum of its human parts – the Irish Empire.

Select Bibliography / Further Reading

The following is a select further-reading list of some of the volumes I leaned on most heavily in the research for *The Irish Empire* and to which I owe a considerable debt.

For the newcomer to the subject of Ireland, *A Concise History* by Máire and Conor Cruise O'Brien (Thames and Hudson, 1997) provides a good pictorial introduction. *The Oxford Illustrated History of Ireland*, edited by R.F. Foster (OUP, 1989) is an excellent thematic cruise past the main landmarks of Irish history and is adorned with very good pictures. Professor Foster's *Modern Ireland 1600–1972* (Allen Lane, 1988) is the standard text for the period. Robert Kee's *The Green Flag Trilogy* (Weidenfeld and Nicholson, 1972) is the classic exploration of the republican movement's development. Early Irish history and its cultural significance for Europe is engagingly treated in Thomas Cahill's *How the Irish Saved Civilization* (Doubleday, 1995).

The history of Irish emigration is now a rich field and is expanding all the time. An indispensable starter text by one of the masters of the subject is Donald Harman Akenson's *The Irish Diaspora – a Primer* (The Institute of Irish Studies, The Queen's University of Belfast, 1997). A central pillar in the edifice of our knowledge is the *Irish World Wide History, Heritage, Identity*, the six-volume study edited by Patrick O'Sullivan (Leicester University Press, 1992–97).

For understanding the phenomenon of Irish emigration to America, Professor Kirby A. Miller's masterly *Emigrants and Exiles* (OUP, 1988) seems unlikely to be surpassed. On the experience of the transatlantic crossing, Terry Coleman's *Passage to America* (Hutchinson, 1972) and Edward Laxton's *The Famine Ships*, (Bloomsbury, 1996) are both enlightening.

On specific aspects of the diaspora, *The New York Irish* edited by Ronald H. Bayor and Timothy J. Meagher (Johns Hopkins, 1996) were both scholarly and entertaining. *Ireland and Irish Australia*, edited by Oliver MacDonagh and W.F. Mandle (Croom Helm, 1986) is a collection of some seminal work on the Irish in the Antipodes. Very useful, too, was *The Irish in the Victorian City* edited by Roger Swift and Sheridan Gilley (Croom Helm, 1985).

For travellers interested in tracking the diaspora in the United States, *Irish American Landmarks* by John A. Barnes (Visible Ink, 1995) provides a comprehensive and fascinating guide.

Picture Acknowledgements

While every effort has been made to trace copyright holders for photographs featured in this book, the publishers will be glad to make proper acknowledgements in future editions of this publication in the event that any regrettable omissions have occurred at the time of going to press.

a = above; b = below

Ancient Art & Architecture Collection: 14 (R.R. Bell), 15a (Brian Wilson), 17, 19 (Cheryl Hogue), 22, 26, 37 (R. Sheridan), 42, 44 (Brian Wilson); The Balch Institute for Ethnic Studies Library: 11 (McGovern Family Photographs), 99 (Howard Applegate Collection); Barnaby's Picture Library: 182; Boston Public Library, Print Department: 106; Bridgeman Art Library: 12 (Marsden Archive), 15b (Royal Geographical Society, London), 21 (Huntington Library & Art Gallery, San Marino), 23 (National Museum of Ireland, Dublin), 25 (Trinity College, Cambridge), 27 (Private Collection), 30 (Fitzwilliam Museum, Cambridge), 31 (Archives National, Paris), 32 (British Library), 33 (Lambeth Palace Library, London), 34 (Private Collection), 35 (British Library), 36 (Private Collection), 38 (Private Collection), 39b (Private Collection), 41 (Private Collection), 43 (Private Collection), 45 (Fine Art Society, London), 48 (Private Collection), 49 (Private Collection), 50 (National Maritime Museum, London), 51 (Private Collection), 52 (Private Collection), 57 (Agnew & Sons, London), 59 (Coram Foundation, London), 63 (Private Collection), 64 (British Museum), 65 (York County Historical Society), 72 (Library of Congress, Washington DC), 73 (Capitol Collection, Washington), 77 (British Museum), 88 (Corcoran Gallery of Art), 101 (Museum of the City of New York), 118 (National Gallery of Scotland, Edinburgh), 121 (Private Collection), 130 (Private Collection), 166 (National Library of Australia, Canberra); Brigman Young University, G.E. Anderson Collection, Harold B. Lee Library: 97; Corbis: 6, 8, 68 (Bojan B), 70a & b, 83a (Bettmann), 84, 92a, 96 (Bettmann), 104, 105b (Bettmann), 107, 108b, 109a, 110, 117, 131, 150 (Bettmann), 153 (Bettmann), 154a (Bettmann), 154b, 155 (Bettmann), 157, 158 (Philip Gould), 159 (Bettmann), 167, 181a & b; Crawford Municipal Gallery, Cork: 81; Edifice: 185b; E.T. Archive: 24, 28, 40, 47a & b, 54; Mary Evans Picture Library: 16 (Arthur Rackham Collection), 29, 39a, 46, 55, 58, 73, 78, 79, 89, 93, 95, 100a & b, 119, 122a, 136, 143a, 165; Fotomas Index: 123, 124, 125, 129; Giraudon: 90; Ronald Grant Archive: 156, 186; William D. Griffin: 10; Robert Harding Picture Library: 134, 139, 140 (Norman Froggatt); John Hillelson Agency: 173 (© Gisèle Freund); Hulton Getty: 66, 67, 71, 75, 87, 91, 94, 105a, 109b, 111a, 126, 132, 133, 135, 143b, 148, 151, 152, 161, 162, 163, 170, 174, 176, 177; Hutchison Picture Library: 13 (© Patricio Goycoolea), 164 (© C. Highes); *Illustrated London News* Picture Library: 83b, 137; Irish Picture Library: half-title page, 85, 102 (Fr. Browne S.J. Collection), 108a, 120 (Leland Duncan Collection), 138 (Fr. Browne S.J. Collection), 141 (Fr. Browne S.J. Collection), 175 (Fr. Browne S.J. Collection); Library of Congress, Washington DC: 98, 111b; National Gallery of Ireland: 82; National Library of Ireland: 92b; Newspix: 180; Popperfoto: 113, 179 (Alan Greeley); Society for the Preservation of New England Antiquities: 103; Sotheby's Transparency Library: 62; Staten Island Historical Society, Alice Austen Collection: 9; Talana Museum, Dundee: 61; Telegraph Colour Library: title page; Tony Stone: 178 (Paul Chesley), 185a (Alain Le Garsoeur); Topham Picturepoint: 80, 122b, 142, 144, 160; Wayne Street University, Archives of Labour and Urban Affairs: 116.

Index